A GUIDE FOR *gentlemen* CHEFS

Published by

NIYOGI BOOKS
D-78, Okhla Industrial Area, Phase-I
New Delhi-110 020, INDIA
Tel: 91-11-26816301, 49327000
Fax: 91-11-26810483, 26813830
email: niyogibooks@gmail.com
www.niyogibooks.com

ISBN: 978-81-89738-33-4
Year of Publication: 2008
Reprint: 2012

Printed at: Niyogi Offset Pvt. Ltd., New Delhi, India

A GUIDE FOR *gentlemen* CHEFS

Laxmi Dhaul
Gitanjali Khanna

Cartoons

Mario Miranda

This book is a humorous attempt to categorise recipes (Indian, Western and Continental) not on the basis of their ingredients or their mode of preparation, but on the varied nature of Gentlemen Chefs. This is all the more relevant today as it is common perception that the best chefs are male and cooking is a hobby that more and more men are taking up. As we all know, cooking is a wonderful stress-reliever!

We have created a substantial number of categories and suggested recipes for each type. Each category contains a tongue-in-cheek verse, and a cartoon by Mario Miranda, reflecting his subtle humorous touch. Please choose the category that you find most apt and select your recipes!!

CONTENTS

Note from the Authors

Beware…finally a handbook for Adam!!!

Both of us are happily married to our respective spouses for decades—no regrets. Both of us have husbands who we think have some culinary talents but nothing worth mentioning. However, the worry lingers of what they would do if they were stranded 'Eve-less' on a lonely island and maybe stumbled on or discovered a readymade, fully equipped kitchen left behind by Robinson Crusoe. Our prayers would be then not only for their safe return to civilization but also that they find this little book and use it as their Man Friday!

Our friendship has spanned many years; it started near the swimming pool of the Bombay Gymkhana where we would spend many sunny afternoons watching our kids learn the breast-stroke and the butterfly-stroke. Sometimes we would discuss recipes; often we just giggled and had fun. Sometimes we were brilliant and planned a cookbook. Our brilliance was in short bursts, interspersed with large helpings of gossip, roasted with our vivid imagination and garnished with our desire to be taken seriously by the 'stronger sex'!! Voilà –the outcome: *A Guide for Gentlemen Chefs.*

The story does not end there; whilst choosing our favourite, easy-to-make, tasty and innovative recipes, we continued to discuss so and so's husband or brother or business colleague and slowly we had a nickname or a category for most of the men we knew or had heard about. The natural outcome was to then sort out the recipes for the various categories of men that we were familiar with! We reiterate that these categories are neither watertight nor final but an attempt on our part to make discreet, tongue-in-cheek suggestions. We had a wonderful compatriot in Mario Miranda who humoured us and in his own very charming way drew the wonderful cartoons from the nonsense verses we penned for each category.

Whilst accepting that the world's greatest chefs are men, you would agree that there exist others who need a little help. We offer this help to them with *A Guide for Gentlemen Chefs*. Often when one looks at portraits of men of history who have left their mark on the sands of time, one wonders what their culinary habits were like or whether they enjoyed cooking. Cooking was never in vogue then but the saying that 'the best way to a man's heart is through his stomach' has been around for centuries. Winston Churchill...hmmm...wonder what category he would have been in: maybe a bully? Albert Einstein, Ernest Hemingway, Napoleon Bonaparte, Pablo Picasso, Vincent Van Gogh...it's not for us to know but only to guess!!

It has been fun writing this book—and we hope you enjoy using it!

Laxmi Dhaul   Gitanjali Khanna

Ode to Gentlemen Chefs

Bachelors, epicureans, gourmets, and such
Savour this book for it offers so much.
It's full of recipes—wondrous and light,
With ambrosial decoctions for that special night!
We cater to one, we cater to all
Be thee grumpy, frumpy or happy and joll!
Be thee married—a blessed state indeed
Or on that front, be thee in need.
Pick out a heading that suits your mood
You may get a shock—but none too rude.
For both bored and intellectual minds
We offer great salads with lemon rinds.
For Mama's boys there are goodies galore
Enjoy them with love while the others snore.
For the happy-go-lucky, the young at heart
We have sandwiches, pinwheels and lemon tart.
The repentant and the almost read
On mega doses of mithai and stew are fed!
We offer these suggestions with humble pride
But request you to take them in your stride!!

How to Cook a 'Wife' Recipe

From the *Yankee Kitchen Cookbook*...author and date unknown, but from the early 1800s

A good many wives are utterly spoilt by mismanagement in cooking and so are not tender and good. Some men keep them constantly in hot water; others let them freeze by their carelessness and indifference. Some keep them in a stew with irritating ways and words. Some husbands keep them pickled, while others waste them shamefully. It cannot be supposed that any wife will be tender and good when so managed, but they are really delicious when prepared properly.

In selecting a wife, you should be guided by the silvery appearance as when buying a mackerel not by the golden tint as if you wanted some salmon. Do not go to the market for her as the best ones are always brought to the door. Be sure to select her yourself as tastes differ. It is far better to have none unless you will patiently learn how to cook her.

Of course, preserving a kettle of the finest porcelain is best, but if you have nothing better than an earthenware pippin, it will do—with a little care. Like crabs and lobsters, wives are cooked alive. Sometimes they fly out of the kettle and do so become burnt and crusty on the edges. So it is wise to secure her in the kettle with a strong silken cord called Comfort. Prepare a clear, steady flame of love, warmth and cheerfulness. Set her as near this as seems to agree with her.

If she sputters, do not be anxious, for some wives do this until they are quite done. Add a little sugar in the form of what confectioners call kisses, but use no pepper or vinegar on any account. Season to taste with spices, good humour and gaiety preferred, but seasoning must always be with great discretion and caution. Avoid sharpness in testing her for tenderness. Stir her gently, lest she lie too flat and close to the kettle and so become useless. You cannot fail to know when she is done. If so treated, you will find her very digestible, agreeing with you perfectly and she will remain that way as long as you choose, unless you become careless and slow the home fires to grow cold. Thus prepared, she will serve a lifetime of happiness!

There was a man who tried to cook,
He found many recipes and took a look,
But often he roasted his fingers brown
As he mistook them for potatoes round,
And in vengeance burnt every cookbook!

BON APPETIT...

For the exotic

(Mughlai cuisine)

The Taj Mahal was built in memory of a queen—
The Mughal emperor left a wonder to be seen!
Their cuisine was rich, with dry fruits and cream
Fragrant and enticing—a badshah's dream!
Try these dishes, come tempt your fate,
Smell and sight are as important as taste!

Mughlai Zaafrani Murgh

(Chicken spiced in saffron, cooked in rich sauces)

Serves: 5-6
Time required: 35 minutes (Marination time: 1 hour)

INGREDIENTS

750 gm chicken, cleaned, washed and cut into pieces
1 teaspoon (tsp) red chilly powder
1 tsp salt
1 tablespoon (tbsp) ginger-garlic paste
2 tbsp yoghurt
4-5 tbsp oil
2-3 bay leaves
4-5 cloves
1 onion, grated
paste of 4-6 cashew nuts soaked overnight
a pinch of saffron soaked in ½ cup warm milk
1 tbsp fresh coriander leaves, chopped

METHOD

1. Mix red chilly powder with a little water, then add salt, ginger-garlic paste, yoghurt and marinate the chicken pieces in it for at least an hour.
2. Heat oil in a pan.
3. Add bay leaves and cloves and stir fry for a minute.
4. Add grated onions and sauté till the smell of raw onion is gone and they are brown.
5. Add the marinated chicken pieces and mix well.
6. Cover and cook for 15 minutes or until the chicken is tender.
7. Add the cashew nut paste and saffron.
8. Mix well.
9. Garnish with freshly chopped coriander. Serve hot.

Nawabi Mutton Pulao

(Exotically spiced meat with fragrant rice)

Serves: 6-8
Time required: 1 hour, 30 minutes

INGREDIENTS

500 gm mutton, cut into small pieces
5 cups *basmati* rice
2 onions,

METHOD

1. Put mutton, roughly chopped onion, salt and 3 cups of water in a heavy-bottomed pan.
2. Bring to a boil.
3. Reduce heat and simmer for approx. 1 hour

roughly chopped
salt to taste
3 cups water
3 tbsp clarified butter
1 large onion,
chopped lengthwise
2 onions, grated
1-inch ginger, grated
1 garlic pod, crushed
1 black cardamom
1-inch stick cinnamon
4 small green cardamoms
½ tsp black cumin seeds
2 cloves
1 bay leaf
4 tsp *kewra*
essence water
a pinch of saffron soaked
in ½ cup warm milk
1 onion, finely sliced

or more, till the meat is almost done.

4. Strain and reserve stock. Keep the mutton and onion pulp aside.
5. Wash rice thoroughly and soak for half-an-hour in cold water.
6. Put 2 tbsp clarified butter in a heavy pan. Fry the onion (chopped lengthwise) till golden.
7. Add the grated onion, ginger, garlic, black cardamom, cinnamon, green cardamoms and black cumin seeds. Fry the mixture till it turns light brown.
8. Add the strained meat and onion pulp.
9. Increase heat and brown meat.
10. Drain the rice well.
11. Add to the meat mixture and fry till rice becomes transparent.
12. Level meat and rice. Add cloves and the bay leaf.
13. Pour the meat stock and top with water to cover rice by 1 inch.
14. Reduce heat, cover rice and cook for approx. 20 minutes or till the meat and rice are nearly cooked.
15. Pour *kewra* essence water and cook covered for another 3-4 minutes.
16. Lift lid and pour in saffron.
17. Cook for another 3-4 minutes.
18. Turn off heat and leave the *pulao* to stand.
19. Gently fork the rice into a serving bowl.
20. In another pan, with the remaining clarified butter, fry the finely sliced onions.
21. Garnish the *pulao* with fried onions. Serve hot.

Shahi Murgh Badami

(Spicy chicken in almond sauce)

Serves: 6-8
Time required: 1 hour

INGREDIENTS

1 kg chicken, skinned and cut into medium-sized pieces
5 tbsp oil
1½ cups blanched almonds, cut into slivers
4-5 onions, finely chopped
8 green cardamoms
2 tsp whole coriander seeds
2 tsp poppy seeds
½ tsp chilly powder
salt to taste
2 cups yoghurt

METHOD

1. Heat 3 tbsp oil in a heavy-bottomed pan.
2. Add chicken and fry till golden. Drain excess oil and keep aside.
3. Add balance 2 tbsp oil and heat.
4. Add almonds and fry till golden. Drain.
5. Lightly brown onions in the same oil.
6. Add almonds (keep aside a few for the garnish), green cardamom, coriander seeds and poppy seeds. Cook for about 5 minutes.
7. Add chilly powder and salt. Stir well and remove from heat.
8. Let the mixture cool, then purée in a blender.
9. Return the purée to the pan and add fried chicken pieces.
10. Cook and coat chicken with the puréed mixture.
11. Add the yoghurt spoon by spoon, stirring after each addition.
12. Cover the pan tightly—reduce heat and let the chicken simmer for about 30 minutes till it turns tender.
13. Let the sauce thicken.
14. Place on platter and sprinkle lightly fried almonds over it. Serve hot.

Roghan Mushroom

(Mushroom in rich tomato sauce)

Serves: 4
Time required: 25 minutes

INGREDIENTS

750 gm mushrooms, stemmed
2 cups water
2 tbsp oil
4 bay leaves
2 cloves
4 green cardamoms
1 black cardamom
1-inch stick of cinnamon
4-5 onions, grated
4 tsp ginger-garlic paste
1½ cups tomato purée
1 tsp chilly powder
1 tsp turmeric powder
2 tsp coriander powder
salt to taste
a pinch of curry powder
1 tbsp fresh coriander leaves, chopped
½-inch ginger, thinly sliced
2 green chillies, finely chopped

METHOD

1. Put mushrooms in a pan. Pour water to cover them. Cook and simmer in low heat for 5 minutes. Drain and keep water aside.
2. Heat oil in a pan. Add bay leaves, cloves, green cardamoms, black cardamom and cinnamon. Sauté till they crackle.
3. Add grated onion and fry till light brown.
4. Stir in ginger-garlic paste, tomato purée, chilly powder, turmeric powder, coriander powder, salt and sauté.
5. Add the mushrooms and then pour in the water kept aside.
6. Cook on low heat till mushrooms are done.
7. Sprinkle a little curry powder, chopped coriander, thinly sliced ginger and green chillies. Serve hot.

Shahi Paneer Baby Corn Korma

(Rich curry of cottage cheese and baby corn)

Serves: 8
Time required: 35 minutes

INGREDIENTS

500 gm cottage cheese cubes
150 gm baby corn
4-5 tbsp oil
1 bay leaf
1 tsp garlic paste
1 large onion, finely grated
2 tomatoes, chopped
6 green chillies, cut lengthwise
2 tsp chilly powder
2 tsp curry powder
a pinch of turmeric powder
1½ cups yoghurt
2 cups water
10 cashew nuts soaked overnight and ground to a fine paste
salt to taste

METHOD

1. Heat oil. Sauté with bay leaf and garlic paste.
2. Add onion and fry till golden.
3. Add tomatoes, green chillies, chilly powder, curry powder, turmeric powder and fry till the oil separates. Add yogurt and simmer for 2 minutes.
4. Add water and bring to a boil.
5. Add cottage cheese cubes, baby corn, cashew nut paste and salt.
6. Simmer for 10-15 minutes on low heat. Serve hot.

Mughlai Keema Matar

(Minced meat and peas in rich sauces)

Serves: 6-8
Time required: 45 minutes

INGREDIENTS

1 kg minced lamb/beef
2 tbsp oil
8 garlic pods, crushed
½-inch ginger, finely chopped
2 onions, finely chopped
1 tsp red chilly powder
1 tsp coriander powder
1 tsp cumin powder
1 tsp curry powder
2 green chillies, finely chopped
2 cups water
1 cup green peas, shelled
1½ tbsp lemon juice
salt to taste

METHOD

1. Heat oil in a pan.
2. Sauté garlic, ginger and onions till the onions turn translucent.
3. Add red chilly powder, coriander powder, cumin powder, curry powder and green chillies.
4. Add the minced meat, stir and cook for 5 minutes.
5. Add water and bring to a boil.
6. Cover pan with a lid and cook on low flame for 30 minutes.
7. Now add peas, lemon juice and salt.
8. Cook until liquid reduces and minced meat is properly cooked. Serve hot.

For the dull-brained

(Fish dishes)

When God created creatures on land
He made sure that food was close at hand.
He made provisions for those momentarily dull
To dive in the sea, to fish like a gull.
Succour is at hand, for those who enquire
How fish is grilled on a charcoal fire:
To poach or bake or even sauté or fry
To cook fish well until the sauces dry.
Try these recipes and impress your friends,
They'll be begging you for the latest trends!

Spicy Fish

Serves: 4-6
Time required: 30 minutes

INGREDIENTS

1 kg surmai, pomfret or ghole, cut into fillets
7 garlic pods
2-inch ginger
2 green chillies
2 red chillies
1 tbsp whole coriander seeds
1 tbsp cumin seeds
1 tsp turmeric powder
3-4 tbsp oil
1 medium-sized onion, finely chopped
5-6 cloves
2 cinnamon sticks (1-inch long)
1 tbsp roasted gram flour
1 tbsp fresh coriander leaves, chopped
salt to taste
2½ cups yoghurt
1 tsp lemon juice

METHOD

1. Grind garlic, ginger, green and red chillies, whole coriander seeds and cumin seeds into a smooth paste.
2. Apply ½ tbsp salt and turmeric to the fish and keep aside.
3. Heat oil in a pan and sauté the fillets lightly. Drain excess oil.
4. In the remaining oil, fry the onion, add ground spices and continue frying till the oil surfaces.
5. Add cloves and cinnamon and fry for another 5 minutes.
6. Add gram flour, ½ tbsp chopped coriander and salt. Add a little water and cook the paste.
7. Put in the fish, add yoghurt and cook till tender.
8. Garnish with the remaining chopped coriander. Sprinkle lemon juice before serving.

Smoked Fish

Serves: 4-6
Time required: 35 minutes (Marination time: 30 minutes)

INGREDIENTS

1 kg pomfret fillet or any firm fish
1 tsp salt
1 tbsp oil
1 tsp tomato sauce
1 tsp anchovy sauce
1 tsp soy sauce
1 tsp chilly sauce
1 tsp Worcestershire sauce
½ cup water
some hay or dried grass
2 cups puffed rice
1 tsp vinegar
1 tsp lemon juice

METHOD

1. Wash the fillet or clean and dry the fish.
2. Rub in salt and oil and keep aside for at least 30 minutes.
3. Mix together all the sauces in a pan. Add water and simmer for 4-5 minutes. Keep aside.
4. Heat coal in a barbecue or charcoal stove till white hot. Put hay on the grid, cover with a layer of puffed rice, and place a grill mesh on top.
5. Put the fish on the mesh and cover with the pan lid to prevent smoke from escaping. Cook fish till tender.
6. Warm the sauce prepared earlier and pour over the fish. Add vinegar and lemon juice and serve.

Salmon Steaks Baked with Mushrooms

Serves: 4-6
Time required: 30 minutes

INGREDIENTS

1 kg salmon steaks
4 tbsp butter or margarine, melted
1 tin mushroom (approx. 115 gm) drained
2 tbsp lemon juice
½ tsp grated lemon rind
1 small onion, grated
salt to taste
pepper
1 tbsp fresh parsley, finely chopped

METHOD

1. Arrange the steaks in a baking dish with the thin ends pointing towards the centre.
2. Mix together butter, mushrooms, lemon juice, grated lemon rind and onion.
3. Spoon it over the salmon.
4. Cover the dish with a cling film. Microwave for 10-12 minutes on high or until the fish flakes easily, or put uncovered under a preheated grill till cooked for 10-15 minutes.
5. Let it stand for 5 minutes, covered. Season with salt and pepper.
6. Garnish with fresh parsley.

Fish in Coconut Milk

Serves: 4-6
Time required: 20 minutes

INGREDIENTS

1 kg fish (ghole)
4 tbsp butter
¾ cup coconut milk
salt to taste

METHOD

1. Cut the fish into 2-inch pieces.
2. Sprinkle with salt.
3. Heat butter in a heavy skillet.
4. Add the fish and sauté till the pieces are brown all over.
5. Add coconut milk.
6. Bring to a boil, season with salt and cook for another 2 minutes.

Fish Chowder

Serves: 3-4
Time required: 45 minutes

INGREDIENTS

500 gm fresh tuna or mackerel
1 tbsp butter
4-5 onions, finely chopped
2-3 potatoes, diced
3 cups boiling water
¼ cup cream
¼ tsp white pepper
¼ tsp powdered ginger
salt to taste

METHOD

1. Cut the fish into small pieces, discarding the skin and bones.
2. Sauté onions in butter till light brown.
3. Add the fish and cook on low heat for 5 minutes.
4. Add the diced potatoes and water.
5. Cover and cook slowly for 30 minutes.
6. Stir in cream and seasonings. Serve hot.

Broiled Fish

Serves: 3-4
Time required: 30 minutes (Marination time: 30-40 minutes)

INGREDIENTS

500 gm fish (shell fish)
1 cup salad oil
1 tbsp parsley
1 tsp oregano
1 tsp chilly powder
½ tsp basil leaves (fresh or powder)
½ tsp garlic paste
salt to taste
1 tbsp oil

METHOD

1. Marinate any fish (or shell fish) for 30-40 minutes with all the ingredients.
2. Keep a little marinade aside and add 1 tbsp oil to it.
3. Broil in an oven or over charcoal.
4. Baste constantly with the remaining marinade.

MAMA!
...

For Mama's boy
(Home delicacies)

That jealous woman, the horrid shrew
Was killing me softly with her stew!
All I wanted was what I ate as I grew,
The way only good old Mama knew.
The torture one had to suffer so far,
Trying exotic dishes from near and afar!
All I want is apple pie, parantha and puri bhaji
All the things she cooked, my darling Ma-ji!

Savoury Sago

Serves: 3-4
Time required: 20 minutes
Standing time to soften sago: overnight

INGREDIENTS

1 cup sago
½ cup crushed and roasted peanuts
1 tsp oil
10-12 fresh curry leaves
1 tsp cumin seeds
3-4 green chillies, finely chopped
1 tsp sugar (adjust to taste)
salt to taste
1 tbsp fresh shredded coconut
1 tbsp fresh coriander leaves, chopped
1 tsp lemon juice

METHOD

1. Wash the sago thoroughly, drain water, and let stand overnight.
2. Remove lumps, if any, from the sago. Each sago must be separate.
3. Mix the sago with peanuts that have been slightly roasted.
4. Heat oil and add curry leaves and cumin seeds. Let them brown a bit. Then add chopped green chillies.
5. Add the sago-peanut mixture and mix well, adding sugar and salt to taste. Be careful not to cover the vessel.
6. Garnish with shredded coconut, coriander and a few drops of lemon juice.

Apple Pie

Serves: 6-8
Time required: 45 minutes (Preparation time: 1½ hours)

INGREDIENTS

For a single crust pie

1¼ cups all-purpose flour
6 tbsp cold unsalted butter, cut into ½-inch cubes
2 tbsp cold vegetable shortening
¼ tsp salt
3-4 tbsp ice water

METHOD

1. Blend together flour, butter, shortening and salt in a bowl with your fingers or a pastry blender till the mixture resembles a pea-sized coarse meal with some small (roughly pea-sized) lumps of butter.
2. Sprinkle 3 tbsp ice water evenly over the mixture and gently stir with a fork until well mixed. Add more ice water (a teaspoon at a time) if necessary.

½ cup water
1 egg, lightly beaten

For the filling

¼ cup all-purpose flour
½ tsp ground cinnamon
¼ tsp ground allspice
⅛ tsp salt
1 cup white sugar
1 kg apples, peeled, cored, and each cut into 10 wedges
1 tbsp fresh lemon juice

3. Add the water gradually while kneading the dough. Turn it out onto a work surface.
4. Divide into 4 portions. Knead each portion once or twice in a forward motion to help distribute fat and press into a ball, then flatten into a 5-inch disc. If the dough is sticky dust lightly with additional flour. Wrap each disk in a plastic wrap and refrigerate until firm for an hour or more.
5. Preheat oven to 200°C.
6. Whisk together flour, cinnamon, allspice, salt, and ⅔ cup sugar in a large bowl. Gently toss in apples and lemon juice.
7. Take out the dough discs from the refrigerator. Knead them together and divide into two portions. Roll each out with a rolling pin into a two 13-inch pastry rounds. Fit one pastry round into a 9-inch pie plate. Trim the edges, leaving about an ½-inch overhang.
8. Spoon the filling into the shell. Cover the pie with the other pastry round, and trim with kitchen shears, leaving an ½-inch overhang. Press edges together, then crimp decoratively. Lightly brush the top of the pie with beaten egg and sprinkle with the remaining sugar.
9. Bake the pie at 150°C for 30 minutes. Cool pie on a rack in warm or room temperature for 2 to 3 hours.

Stuffed Potato Parantha

(Indian whole wheat flat bread stuffed with potato and pan fried)

Serves: 6-8

Time required: 35 minutes (Time required to soften dough: 2-3 hours)

INGREDIENTS

3 cups wheat flour
salt to taste
clarified butter
or oil to fry
4 small potatoes, boiled
½-inch ginger, grated
1 tbsp fresh coriander
leaves, chopped
½ tsp red chilly powder
2 green chillies,
finely chopped

METHOD

1. Mix flour, a pinch of salt and 1 tbsp oil. Knead the flour with sufficient water to make a soft dough. Keep covered for at least 2-3 hours.
2. Mash potatoes while still hot and add grated ginger, fresh coriander, red chilly powder, green chillies, salt and mix well. Set aside.
3. Divide the mashed potato into balls.
4. Divide the dough into golf-sized balls, twice the number in step 3. Taking out two balls at a time, roll into two *chapati*s using a little oil instead of flour (this will make the *parantha*s crisp).
5. Take a ball of the mashed potato, spread evenly on one *chapati,* and cover with the other. Seal the edges firmly all around by pressing them with wet fingers.
6. Heat a skillet, put in the *parantha* and after a few minutes gently flip it. Now add oil or clarified butter all around the edges till the *parantha* is evenly brown, then turn the side over once again till both sides are cooked. Serve immediately.

Stuffed Egg Parantha

(Indian whole wheat flat bread stuffed with egg and pan fried)

Serves: 6-8
Time required: 35 minutes (Time required to soften dough: 2-3 hours)

INGREDIENTS

3 cups wheat flour
4 eggs, beaten
½ tsp turmeric powder
salt to taste
1 cup chopped onions or shallots
2 green chillies, finely chopped
½-inch ginger, grated
½ tsp red chilly powder
1 tbsp fresh coriander leaves, chopped
clarified butter or oil to fry

METHOD

1. Beat the eggs thoroughly, with a pinch of turmeric and salt.
2. Fry the chopped onions, green chillies and ginger till the onions turn brown.
3. Add red chilly powder, eggs and salt. Cook, stirring all the while, until the eggs are done. Add coriander and mix well. Keep aside.
4. Divide the dough (see Step 1 of recipe on facing page) into golf-sized balls. Taking 2 balls at a time, roll into 2 *chapati*s using a little oil instead of flour (to make the *parantha*s crisp).
5. Take a spoon of the egg mixture, spread evenly on one *chapati,* and cover with the other. Seal the edges firmly all around by pressing them with wet fingers.
6. Heat a skillet, put in the *parantha* and after a few minutes gently flip it. Now add oil or clarified butter all around the edges until it gets evenly brown, then turn the side over once again till both sides are cooked. Serve immediately.

Potato Curry

Serves: 4-5
Time required: 35 minutes

INGREDIENTS

500 gm potatoes
4 tbsp oil
1 tsp mustard seeds
1½ tsp lentil
2-3 onions, chopped
6 green chillies, finely chopped
1-inch ginger, finely chopped
2 sprigs curry leaves
½ tsp chilly powder
½ tsp turmeric powder
1½ tsp black gram, boiled
1½ tsp Bengal gram, boiled
salt to taste
1 tbsp fresh coriander leaves, chopped
2 tbsp gram flour
¾ cup water
juice of 1 lemon

METHOD

1. Boil and peel the potatoes. Cut into small pieces.
2. Heat oil and add mustard seeds. When they start crackling, add the lentil and fry until golden in colour. Add onions, chillies, ginger, curry leaves, chilly powder and turmeric. Fry until the onions are brown.
3. Add the potatoes, black gram, Bengal gram, salt and chopped coriander and mix thoroughly. Fry for another minute or two.
4. Mix the gram flour with ¾ cup water and add to the curry. Simmer for a couple of minutes. Remove from fire and add lemon juice. Mix well, return to the fire, and simmer till desired thickness.

Note: If a dry curry is preferred, omit the last step. Instead of gram flour, add lemon juice to the curry along with some fresh coriander leaves.

Puri (Puffy deep-fried Indian whole wheat bread)

Serves: 6-8
Time required: 35 minutes

INGREDIENTS

2½ cups wheat flour
3 tsp oil for the dough
salt to taste
½ cup water
oil to fry
½ cup white flour
for dusting the puris

METHOD

1. Mix wheat flour, oil and a pinch of salt with water and knead it to form a stiff dough. Add more water if required.
2. Roll out into *puri*s (circular-shaped bread) about 6-7 cms in diameter on a flour board.
3. Deep fry the *puri*s to a golden colour, turning over once they puff up. Serve immediately with potato curry (see recipe on facing page).

MEAT! GIVE ME MEAT!

For the bloodthirsty

(Steaks)

Chicken steak, fish steak, beef steak dear,
Well cooked, uncooked, cubed, raw and clear!
For the bloodthirsty kings of kings
Who after battle, retreat to the wings.
Try a Chateaubriand or a steak with sauce:
Pepper, garlic, radish red or horse
With a steak, take the world in your stride
Add a dash of seasoning and smile with pride.
Not everyone can perform such a feat
To make a sumptuous dish from red meat!

Steak Creole

Serves: 4-5
Time required: 40 minutes

INGREDIENTS

750 gm steak
4 tbsp butter
2 onions, sliced
several celery sticks, finely chopped
4-5 tomatoes, skinned, chopped and mixed with 2 cups of meat stock
salt and pepper to taste
boiled noodles or rice

METHOD

1. Cut the steak into finger-sized pieces and toss into hot butter.
2. Add onions and celery.
3. Now add chopped tomatoes mixed in meat stock, salt and pepper. Simmer for 30 minutes till tender.
4. Serve on a bed of noodles or rice.

Marchand de Vin Sauce

Serves: 5-6
Time required: 15 minutes

INGREDIENTS

4 tbsp butter
6 scallions (or onions), minced
½ cup red wine
1 cup (or can) beef gravy
1 tbsp lemon juice

METHOD

1. Melt 2 tbsp butter in a pan. Add the minced scallions or onions.
2. Cook for 5 minutes.
3. Add red wine and simmer for 5 minutes.
4. Add beef gravy and the lemon juice.
5. Before serving, heat slowly and add the remaining butter.

Beefy Joes

Serves: 5-6
Time required: 35 minutes

INGREDIENTS

500 gm ground lamb/beef
1 tbsp chopped celery
1-2 onions, chopped
1¼ cups stock (or beef gravy)
¼ cup ketchup
salt to taste
4 hamburger buns

METHOD

1. In a skillet, brown the ground meat with chopped celery and onion.
2. Add stock or gravy, ketchup and salt.
3. Cook over low heat for 15-20 minutes, stirring occasionally, till the meat is tender.
4. Serve over split buns.

Steak Supreme

Serves: 5-6
Time required: 50 minutes (Marination time: 1-2 hours)

INGREDIENTS

6 steaks, ¾-inch thick
3 tbsp Bourbon barbecue sauce for marinating
6-7 garlic pods, crushed
½ tsp tenderizing powder (optional)
1 tbsp butter
salt to taste

METHOD

1. An hour before cooking, coat the steaks with Bourbon barbecue sauce and sprinkle crushed garlic. Marinate for 1-2 hours. If necessary, tenderize with tenderizing powder.
2. Brush the steaks with butter. Add salt. Broil till brown—about 10 minutes for each side.
3. Preheat oven to 200°C. Roast the steaks in oven at 180°C till done (check after 5-10 minutes by cutting the centre of the steaks). It should be medium rare.

For the almost gone
(Nourishing meals)

The Irish believed in leprechauns and magic
Even though it defied all logic,
But the legacy they have left behind
of Irish stew will blow your mind.
Make stew with vegetables, potatoes or mutton
with dumplings enough to feed a glutton!
Lagansala, a Parsi dish sweet and sour
suits all moods:happy and dour
Dal gosht or Dhansak is a Sunday treat
With lentils, rice, veggies and meat!

Chicken Dhansak

(Chicken in aromatic Parsi spices and lentils)

Serves: 5-6
Time required: 1 hour (Soaking time to soften lentils: 2-3 hours)

INGREDIENTS

500 gm chicken breast pieces
⅓ cup yellow split pea lentil *(toovar dal)*
⅓ cup yellow split lentils *(moong dal)*
⅓ cup yellow lentils *(masoor dal)*
2 tbsp clarified butter or oil
2 onions, sliced
4 pods garlic, crushed
1-inch fresh ginger, finely chopped
6 dry red chillies
1-inch cinnamon stick
2 green cardamoms, crushed
4 black peppercorns
½ tsp turmeric powder
1 tbsp coriander powder
1 tsp cumin powder
2 large tomatoes, chopped
1 medium aubergine, cut into 4 pieces
100 gm red pumpkin, peeled and cut into 4 pieces
1 cup fenugreek leaves, fresh or dried
6 cups water

METHOD

1. Soak all the lentils together in cold water for 2-3 hours.
2. Heat oil and fry the onions till brown. Add garlic, ginger, red chillies, cinnamon, green cardamoms, peppercorns, turmeric, coriander and cumin powder. Cook for 5 minutes.
3. Add chopped tomatoes and cook for another 5 minutes. Then add the chicken pieces and cook till dry. Add the three types of lentils, aubergine, pumpkin and fenugreek leaves. Mix well.
4. Slowly add 6 cups of water and salt. Bring to a boil. Cover and simmer on low heat till the chicken is cooked. Remove from fire and keep aside.
5. Soak tamarind in ½ cup boiling water for 15 minutes.
6. Strain the liquid through a sieve and extract all the juices. Discard the pulp.
7. Remove the chicken from the lentils and keep aside.
8. Mash the lentils through a colander into another pan.
9. Then mix with the chicken again.
10. Add the tamarind juice, *Dhansak masala* and jaggery to the chicken/lentils and cook slowly for another 10 minutes. Add extra water if too thick.
11. Fry the finely chopped onion and sprinkle on top together with chopped coriander before serving. Serve with *roti* or rice.

1 tbsp tamarind pulp
½ cup boiling water
readymade *Dhansak masala*
1 tbsp grated jaggery
1 onion, finely chopped
1 tbsp fresh coriander leaves, chopped
2½ tsp salt

Note: Dhansak *masala* is a special type of spice available in stores usually run by Parsis.

Traditionally, Dhansak is served with brown rice where about 2 tbsp of brown caramelized sugar is added to the rice while it is being cooked.

Dal Gosht (Spicy meat and lentil curry)

Serves: 6-8 (Soaking time to soften lentils: 2-3 hours)
Time required: 1 hour (Marination time: 1 hour)

INGREDIENTS

1 kg beef/lamb, cubed
1 tbsp ginger-garlic paste
1 cup gram *(channa)* dal
½ cup yellow split pea lentil *(toovar dal)*
½ cup red lentils *(masoor)*
2 tbsp rice
2 onions, finely chopped
2 sticks cinnamon
1 black cardamom
4 cloves
1 tbsp oil
1 tomato, finely chopped
1 tsp turmeric powder
1 tsp red chilly powder
1 tsp curry powder
salt to taste
1 tbsp fresh coriander
a few leaves of fresh green mint

METHOD

1. Marinate the meat in ginger-garlic paste for 1 hour.
2. Soak the lentils and rice in warm water for about an hour.
3. Cook lentils and rice with half of the chopped onion, cinnamon, black cardamom, cloves and a pinch of turmeric powder till the mixture is soft.
4. Heat oil and fry the remaining onion.
5. Add chopped tomato and sauté with the onions.
6. Add turmeric powder, red chilly powder, curry powder, salt and mix well. Add the marinated meat, 2 cups of water and cook till the meat is tender.
7. Add in the cooked lentil mixture and let it simmer with the meat for about half-an-hour.
8. Garnish with chopped coriander and mint leaves.

Irish Stew

Serves: 5-6
Time required: 1 hour

INGREDIENTS

500 gm beef/lamb, cut into small pieces
2 tbsp butter
a bunch of celery (optional)
2-3 cloves
1 large black cardamom
1-inch cinnamon
salt to taste
¾ litre water, more can be added
3 large carrots, cut in rounds
100 gm beans, threaded and cut into ½-inch pieces
100 gm cauliflower, cut into florets
2 medium-sized onions, cut into 4 pieces
2 whole peeled potatoes, cut into quarters
1 tbsp flour or corn flour
½ cup milk
pepper to taste

METHOD

1. Heat butter in a frying pan. Add meat pieces and sauté lightly.
2. Transfer meat into a casserole. Add celery, cloves, black cardamom, cinnamon, salt and water. Let it simmer covered till the meat is done.
3. Add carrots, beans, cauliflower, onions and potatoes to the cooked meat.
4. Cook together till the vegetables are soft but firm and the mutton is tender.
5. Either mix flour in a little milk or corn flour in a little water, and stir into the stew. Allow it to thicken. Add pepper. Serve hot.

Lagansala

(Vegetables cooked in spicy gravy)

Serves: 5-6
Time required: 30 minutes

INGREDIENTS

100 gm carrots, cubed
2 sweet potatoes, cubed
100 gm French beans, cubed
100 gm green peas
2 medium potatoes, cubed
3 big tomatoes, finely chopped
2 medium-sized onions, finely chopped
1 tsp ginger-garlic paste
2-3 cardamoms
2 cloves
1-inch cinnamon stick
½ tsp turmeric powder
½ tsp chilly powder
½ tsp cumin powder
½ tsp coriander powder
salt to taste
2½ tsp sugar
3 tbsp vinegar
1 tbsp fresh coriander leaves, finely chopped

METHOD

1. Sauté each vegetable separately and keep aside.
2. Purée tomatoes in a blender.
3. Fry onions till they become translucent. Add ginger-garlic paste and cook over medium heat.
4. Pound cardamoms, cloves and cinnamon together and put into the pan.
5. Add turmeric, chilly powder, cumin powder and coriander powder and fry well (if the powdered spices stick to the pan, add a little water).
6. Add the puréed tomatoes, salt, sugar and vinegar. Add fried vegetables and cook for a while.
7. Serve hot garnished with fresh coriander.

G-R-R-R
BY CHRISTOP

For the sailor

(Seafood specialities)

For the truly inspired but aspiring behold
Advice is free, not to be sold!
Try crabs and shell fish found offshore
The lady will beg 'No more, No more!!'
A bite of prawns, scallops and bacon
is more than enough to ignite passion.
Lobsters and crabs: hot, spicy or plain
Watch the population rise, the census gain!

Crab au Gratin

Serves: 5-6
Time required: 55 minutes

INGREDIENTS

2 cups chopped crab meat
3 tbsp butter
2 tbsp white flour
3 tbsp milk
1 cup grated cooking cheese
salt to taste
1 tbsp crushed black pepper

METHOD

1. Steam the crab meat. Transfer it to a non-stick broiling pan.
2. To prepare the white sauce, melt butter in a pan over slow fire. Add white flour and allow it to become slightly brown. Now add milk stirring continuously till the white sauce thickens.
3. Add about ½ cup cooking cheese and salt to the white sauce.
4. Now pour the white sauce over the crab meat. Sprinkle black pepper on top and cover with the rest of the grated cooking cheese.
5. Broil for 20 minutes in high heat.

If ready crab meat is not available, follow these instructions to dress fresh boiled crab still in its shell.

1. Pull off all the pincers and wipe the shell.
2. Turn the crab on its back and extract the meat from its shell. Retain the shell to serve the meat in (optional).
3. Remove and discard stomach bag and grey fingers (these are not edible).
4. Take out all the meat.
5. Crack the top of the shell and remove pieces to make a cavity for the filling.
6. If the crabs have large pincers, these can be cracked and the meat from them extracted and added to the meat from the shell.

Prawn Cocktail

Serves: 5-6
Time required: 20 minutes (Chilling time: 1 hour)

INGREDIENTS

2 cups deveined boiled prawns or shrimps
3 tbsp thick mayonnaise
a few drops of tabasco sauce
1 tbsp Worcestershire sauce
1 tbsp tomato ketchup
2 tbsp full cream (optional)
½ tsp celery powder or 1 stalk of fresh celery, chopped
2 tbsp leeks, finely chopped
1 tsp lemon juice
salt and pepper to taste
3-4 lettuce leaves, finely shredded
5-6 lemon slices

METHOD

1. To make the sauce, mix mayonnaise, tabasco sauce, Worcestershire sauce, tomato ketchup and full cream.
2. Mix the sauce with celery powder or chopped fresh celery, finely chopped leeks and a dash of lemon juice.
3. Season with salt and pepper.
4. Arrange the lettuce leaves in glasses or small flat dishes.
5. Place the boiled prawns or shrimps on the lettuce.
6. Cover with the sauce and garnish with the lemon slices. Refrigerate for at least 1 hour. Serve chilled.

Lobster Thermidor

Serves: 3-4
Time required: 45 minutes

INGREDIENTS

meat of 2 medium-sized lobsters
2 tbsp butter
2 cups flour
1 cup milk
2 tbsp thick cream
salt and pepper to taste
1 small onion, finely chopped
2 tbsp white wine or sherry
1 tbsp grated cheese (preferably Parmesan)

METHOD

1. Boil the lobster meat. Dice into small pieces.
2. Make white sauce with 2 tsp butter, flour, milk, cream, salt and pepper.
3. Add the diced lobster meat and heat gently stirring constantly. Remove from heat.
4. In a separate saucepan, heat the remaining butter. Lightly sauté the onion.
5. Add the sautéed onions to the diced lobster and white sauce together with wine or sherry and mix well.
6. Transfer the lobster meat into lobster shells (if available) or into a non-stick tray.
7. Sprinkle grated cheese and place under a hot grill for 10-15 minutes till the cheese turns brown. Serve hot.

Scallops and Bacon

Serves: 4
Time required: 15 minutes

INGREDIENTS

4 scallops
salt and pepper to taste
1 tsp lemon juice
4 rashers of bacon

METHOD

1. Remove scallops from their shells. Discard the shells.
2. Season scallops with salt and pepper. Add lemon juice.
3. Wrap each soft scallop in a bacon rasher.
4. Secure onto skewers by placing 3 to 4 rashers on one skewer, depending on the quantity.
5. Grill for 5 minutes.

For those crazy about eggs

(Egg dishes)

Anyone can cook an egg, it is simple and easy
We have tasty recipes—classy as well as 'cheesy'
Do you know that these recipes hold magic?
Follow them with spirit, élan and chic.
And do you know what the outcome will be?
Success at last, supreme victory!
Impress your lady love's choice of cheese
In a soufflé, a quiche or an omelette please.
Avoid eggs fried, poached or boiled,
For desire may dry up, the libido foiled!

Curried Scrambled Eggs

Serves: 4
Time required: 25 minutes

INGREDIENTS

4 eggs
4 tbsp oil
1 medium-sized onion, sliced
1 green chilly, chopped
1 firm tomato, chopped into small pieces
½ tsp chilly powder
½-inch ginger, grated
3-4 garlic pods, diced
salt and pepper to taste
1 tbsp coriander leaves, finely chopped

METHOD

1. Heat the oil in a saucepan and fry the onion till soft.
2. Add green chillies and tomato and stir fry over slow heat for about a minute.
3. Add chilly powder, grated ginger and diced garlic, and continue stirring for 3-5 minutes.
4. Break the eggs separately into a bowl and whisk, seasoning with salt and pepper.
5. Reduce the heat and slowly pour the egg batter into the saucepan stirring continuously till the curried scrambled eggs take shape.
6. Sprinkle fresh coriander on top and serve hot with toast or Indian bread—*naan* or *chapati*s.
7. Serve either as a side dish at breakfast or brunch, or as a quick snack.

Eggs Benedictine

Serves: 8
Time required: 25 minutes

INGREDIENTS

8 eggs, poached
1 tbsp butter
8 ham slices
4 English muffins,
split and toasted
1 tbsp parsley, chopped

For Hollandaise sauce

3 egg yolks
¾ cup melted butter
½ tsp lemon juice
cayenne pepper to taste
salt to taste

METHOD

1. To poach the eggs, boil water in a shallow pan, add a little salt and then break each egg and slowly let it slide into the water.
2. Remove the eggs with a ladle when cooked. Put aside and drain.
3. For the Hollandaise sauce, place 3 egg yolks in a stainless steel bowl over steam or in a double boiler over boiling water.
4. Gradually add melted butter, lemon juice and seasonings.
5. Cook only until it thickens. Do not over cook.
6. Fry the ham slices in 1 tbsp butter, on both sides, then place each on top of one half-slice toasted English muffin.
7. Put a poached egg on top of the ham slice and cover with the Hollandaise sauce.
8. Garnish with chopped parsley.

Devilled Eggs

Serves: 6
Time required: 25 minutes

INGREDIENTS

6 hard-boiled eggs
2 tbsp mayonnaise
1 tbsp French dressing
1 tbsp cream
1 tbsp butter
salt to taste
½ tsp paprika
½ tsp dry mustard (optional)
1 tbsp parsley, chopped
1 tbsp chives
1 tbsp olives, finely sliced
anchovies (optional)
few capers

METHOD

1. Shell the hard-boiled eggs. Cut them in halves and remove the yolks.
2. Crush the yolks with a fork and make them into a smooth paste with mayonnaise, French dressing, cream and butter.
3. Season the paste with salt, paprika and dry mustard.
4. Fill the egg whites with the paste and garnish the eggs with chopped parsley or chives, sliced olives, anchovies, capers, etc.

A variation is deep-fried devilled eggs:

Beat an egg well, dip the devilled eggs into it, then roll over fine bread crumbs and deep fry till brown. Serve immediately.

Scotch Eggs

Serves: 4
Time required: 35 minutes

INGREDIENTS

5 eggs, 4 hard-boiled and shelled
500 gm minced meat (lamb/beef/pork)
1 tbsp fresh parsley, chopped
1 onion, grated
¼ tsp ground cinnamon
⅛ tsp ground nutmeg
1½ tsp salt
1 tsp pepper
1 cup white flour
½ cup fine and dry bread crumbs
3-4 lettuce leaves, washed

METHOD

1. Add parsley, onion, cinnamon, nutmeg, salt and pepper to the minced meat. Mix well.
2. Divide the meat mixture into 4 portions and shape into patties.
3. Beat 1 egg and keep aside.
4. Roll the hard-boiled eggs over the white flour sifted with salt and pepper.
5. Place one shelled hard-boiled egg on top of each patty.
6. Shape the minced meat mixture around the egg till it is completely covered.
7. Now dip it into the beaten egg.
8. Roll over the dry bread crumbs and deep fry to a golden brown. Cut into halves lengthwise.
9. Serve on a bed of lettuce.

Soufflé Eggs on Vegetable Base

Serves: 2
Time required: 40 minutes

INGREDIENTS

2 eggs
2 tbsp oil
1 large onion, chopped
2 green chillies, chopped
1 tsp ginger-garlic paste
1 tomato, chopped
½ tsp coriander powder
½ tsp cumin powder
1 tbsp coriander, finely chopped
salt to taste
2 potatoes, half-boiled and sliced into thick rounds

METHOD

1. Heat oil in a skillet. Add onion, green chillies, ginger-garlic paste, tomato, coriander and cumin powder, chopped coriander and salt. Fry for a while.
2. Now add in the potatoes and cook covered over a slow fire till the potatoes are done.
3. Spread the above mixture while hot in a flat fire-proof serving dish.
4. Separate the egg whites and yolks. Beat the egg whites till stiff and the egg yolks lightly. Then fold the egg yolks gently in the whites and spread over the mixture.
5. Bake in a preheated oven at 205°C for 20 minutes till the top is golden brown.

Note: Instead of potatoes, you can use other vegetables like carrots, French beans, etc., for the base.

From the Parsis—Lady Finger Eggs

Serves: 5
Time required: 30 minutes

INGREDIENTS

¼ kg okra,
sliced into rounds
2 eggs
3 tbsp oil
2 onions, chopped
¼ tsp turmeric powder
1 tsp chilly powder
salt to taste

METHOD

1. Heat oil and fry onion till golden. Now add turmeric powder and chilly powder. Drain the excess oil.
2. Add okra. Cover and simmer on slow fire for 5 minutes till okra is tender. Season with salt.
3. Separate the egg whites and yolks. Beat the egg whites till stiff. Whisk the yolks lightly and blend into the whites.
4. Spread over the okra mix in the same frying pan. Cover and cook for 2-3 minutes till the egg batter is set. Serve hot.

SPINACH
O-O-O
WOW!

For the weak

(Spinach dishes)

Popeye the sailor, the 'spinach star'
Showed kids that magic was not far.
A bunch of green leaves, nonetheless
As a source of power was one of the best!
Try it in the dishes mentioned here
In recipes collected from far and near,
In soufflés, salads or with cottage cheese
We promise instant power right down to your knees!

Spinach Soufflé

Serves: 4
Time required: 1 hour

INGREDIENTS

2 cups fresh spinach, leaves washed and destemmed
1 onion, chopped
1-inch stick cinnamon
½ tsp ground nutmeg
2 tbsp butter
2 tsp flour
1 cup milk
¼ cup grated cheese
salt to taste
½ tsp ground pepper
3 eggs

METHOD

1. Steam together the spinach, onion, cinnamon and nutmeg. Cool, remove the cinnamon stick and blend the mixture finely.
2. In a saucepan, melt butter. Add flour and sauté lightly. Add milk and make a thick white sauce. Put in the spinach purée and cheese and cook till the cheese has melted. Add salt and pepper.
3. Separate the egg whites and yolks. Beat the egg whites till stiff and yolks till creamy.
4. Add to the spinach mix. Fold in the egg whites.
5. Pour into soufflé moulds and bake in 205°C for 45 minutes or till well risen. Serve hot.

Shredded Chicken, Bacon and Spinach

Serves: 5-6
Time required: 35 minutes

INGREDIENTS

400 gm chicken, shredded and cooked
2 bacons slices
1¼ kg spinach
2 tbsp butter
1 chicken cube
3½ tbsp soy sauce
1½ tsp sugar
2 tbsp sherry
salt and pepper to taste
3-4 spring onions, sliced
3 cups steamed noodles

METHOD

1. Wash and stem the spinach. Heat 1 tbsp butter. Add spinach and cook for 1½ minutes.
2. Sprinkle the chicken cube over the spinach. Add soy sauce, sugar, sherry, salt, pepper and cook for 3-4 minutes.
3. Heat 1 tbsp butter in another pan. Add bacon slices and fry crisply. Add shredded cooked chicken and spring onion and stir fry.
4. Transfer these into the spinach mix. Mix well. Serve with steamed noodles.

Cottage Cheese in Spinach

Serves: 5-6
Time required: 35 minutes

INGREDIENTS

200 gm cottage cheese, cut into cubes
400 gm spinach
2 tbsp oil
3 tomatoes, sliced
1½ tsp coriander powder
1 tsp cumin powder
chilly powder to taste
2-3 green chillies, slit lengthwise
salt to taste

METHOD

1. Clean and blanch the spinach leaves in a small quantity of water. Cool and purée the spinach into a paste.
2. Heat oil and fry the cubed cottage cheese lightly. Remove the cubes, drain the oil on absorbent paper and keep aside.
3. Add sliced tomatoes and salt to the oil and fry for about 5 minutes till it is mashed.
4. Add coriander, cumin and chilly powder and cook for another 5 minutes over low flame.
5. Stir in the spinach purée, mixing evenly.
6. Add the fried cheese cubes and simmer for about 2-3 minutes.
7. Garnish with green chillies.

Spinach with Mushroom Salad

Serves: 5-6
Time required: 20 minutes (Chilling time: 20 minutes)

INGREDIENTS

2 heads of spinach
8-10 mushrooms, fresh or tinned

For the salad dressing

6 garlic pods
1 tbsp vinegar
1 tbsp honey
1 tbsp olive oil
½ tsp black pepper
salt to taste

METHOD

1. Steam the spinach and keep the leaves whole. Stem the mushrooms and cut into halves.
2. For the salad dressing, mix garlic, vinegar, honey, olive oil, ground black pepper, salt and shake in a jar.
3. Lay out the spinach and mushrooms in a shallow bowl.
4. Pour the dressing over it. Mix and refrigerate. Serve cold.

For the henpecked
(Chicken dishes)

If you are one of those, let's say,
Whose 'pecked' on, forever and a day,
Tell your beloved, to hold her ire
Chicken dishes are what you desire!
You'll spend your life, happy—not wreck'd
So eat your chicken, content and henpecked!

Chicken Curry in Coconut Cream

Serves: 4
Time required: 20 minutes (Marination time: 30 minutes)

INGREDIENTS

4 chicken breasts, boneless, skinned and cut into 2-3 inch pieces
2 tbsp lemon juice
3 tbsp sesame oil
2 medium-sized onions, finely sliced
4 garlic pods, finely sliced
1-inch ginger, cut thin
2 green chillies, finely chopped
1 tbsp sesame seed
3 cloves
1-inch cinnamon stick
salt to taste
¼ litre thick coconut milk
¼ litre thin coconut milk
1 tbsp fresh coriander leaves, finely chopped

METHOD

1. Marinate the chicken breasts in lemon juice and a pinch of salt for half an hour
2. Heat the oil. Add the chicken pieces and fry till golden brown.
3. Remove the chicken pieces, drain, and keep aside.
4. Add the onions, garlic, ginger, green chillies, sesame seed, cloves and cinnamon. Reduce heat and stir often till the onion becomes pale golden in colour.
5. Add salt and both the thick and thin coconut milk and stir well. Bring to a boil.
6. Now add the chicken pieces. Mix well.
7. Cook uncovered for 10 minutes, stirring often till the chicken is tender and the sauces thicken.
8. Sprinkle with fresh coriander and serve hot.

Note: Thick coconut milk is the milk extracted from freshly shredded coconut; thin coconut milk is obtained when the shredded coconut is then soaked in water and pressed for further milk. The other option is to use coconut cream, available in tins or tetrapacks.

Anise Chicken

Serves: 5-6
Time required: 1 hour

INGREDIENTS

4 chicken breasts
4 chicken drumsticks
2 tbsp butter
8 small white onions (either scallions or regular ones), chopped
2 cups fresh mushrooms, washed and quartered
⅓ cup flour
1 tbsp oil
1 cup tomato purée
2 tomatoes, blanched and chopped
1½ cups chicken broth made with stock or chicken bouillon cube
¼ cup dry white wine or sherry
1 tsp sweet basil, finely chopped
½ tsp anise seed
salt to taste
2 cups peas

METHOD

1. Sauté onions and mushrooms in ½ tbsp butter. Set aside.
2. Heat the remaining butter and oil. Dust the chicken with flour and fry till golden. Add onions and mushrooms to the chicken pieces together with tomato purée, chopped tomatoes, broth or stock, wine, basil, anise seeds and salt.
3. Stir. Bring to a boil and simmer.
4. Reduce heat and cook covered for 30 minutes till the chicken is tender.
5. Add peas. Stir and cook for another 15 minutes. Serve with green salad, bread rolls and a bottle of Vin Rosé.

Chicken Satay

Serves: 6-8
Time required: 20 minutes (Marination time: 1-2 hours)

INGREDIENTS

4 boneless chicken breasts, cut into broad long strips

For the marinade

1 tbsp soy sauce
1 tbsp oil
1 tsp red chilly powder
salt to taste
2 tbsp lemon juice

For the peanut sauce

1 tbsp oil
4 garlic pods, chopped
1 onion, grated
¼ cup roasted peanuts, powdered
3 tbsp tomato purée
2 tsp honey
1 tbsp soy sauce
1 tsp red chilly powder
salt to taste
1 cup water

METHOD (for the satay)

1. Mix the marinade ingredients and add to the chicken strips. Marinate for 1-2 hours.
2. Pierce the marinated chicken onto wooden skewers or skewers made of sugarcane sticks (if available).
3. Grill for 10 minutes, or grease a non-stick pan slightly and cook on both sides. Sprinkle lemon juice.
4. Serve with peanut sauce.

For the sauce:

5. Heat oil in pan. Add chopped garlic and grated onion.
6. Cook on high heat for 1 minute, stirring continuously.
7. Now add powdered peanuts, tomato purée, honey, soy sauce, chilly powder, salt and water.
8. Bring to a boil. Simmer for a few minutes.

Chicken Fruity

Serves: 5-6
Time required: 1 hour (Marination time: 30 minutes)

INGREDIENTS

1 kg chicken, breasts and thighs cut into medium-sized pieces
4 tbsp lemon juice
¼ cup flour
1½ tsp salt
¼ tsp black pepper
3 tbsp butter
3 tbsp olive oil
1 large onion, chopped
1 cup pineapple slices, crushed and drained
3 medium tomatoes, diced
3 tbsp black currants (optional)
2 tbsp brown sugar
4 tbsp rum
3 cups noodles, steamed

METHOD

1. Apply lemon juice and ½ tsp salt to the chicken pieces and keep aside for at least 30 minutes.
2. Coat the chicken pieces with flour (seasoned with ¼ tsp salt and black pepper).
3. Heat butter. Fry the chicken pieces and keep aside.
4. Heat oil in another pan and add onion. Cook for 5 minutes, stirring occasionally.
5. Add pineapple slices, diced tomatoes, black currants, salt and brown sugar.
6. Mix well and let it simmer on low heat for 30 minutes.
7. Pour in the rum.
8. Serve over steamed noodles.

For today's Casanova
(Pasta dishes)

For the Casanovas who amongst us hide,
We do have menus, we must confide.
Simple, easy-to-make, with no time to waste—
Tomatoes, garlic, a little imagination and taste.
Choose your recipe, maybe a pasta delight?
But to impress, get the ingredients just right!

Macaroni with Minced Meat

Serves: 3-4
Time required: 1 hour

INGREDIENTS

2 cups macaroni
500 gm mutton, minced
2 tbsp butter
2 onions, chopped
½ cup tomato purée
1 tsp salt
½ tsp fresh ground black pepper
a pinch each of cinnamon powder, oregano powder and nutmeg powder
1 tbsp flour
1½ cup milk
¼ cup cream
2 egg yolks, lightly beaten
½ cup freshly grated cheese

METHOD

1. Preheat oven to 200°C.
2. Cook the macaroni in 4 cups of water with a pinch of salt till firm, but tender. Drain and rinse under cold water.
3. Heat 1 tbsp butter and fry the onion till brown.
4. Add minced meat. Stir and cook till browned.
5. Add tomato purée, salt, pepper, cinnamon, oregano and nutmeg.
6. Melt the remaining butter in another saucepan and stir in the flour.
7. Pour milk, stirring constantly till the liquid is thick and smooth.
8. Combine cream with the 2 beaten egg yolks. Stir in the sauce. Do not boil.
9. In a baking dish, place a layer of macaroni
10. and cover with a layer of meat. Pour the cream sauce and sprinkle cheese over it. Bake for 30–35 minutes.
    Remove from the oven. Slice into large
11. squares and serve lukewarm.

Spaghetti Bolognaise

Serves: 3-4
Time required: 45 minutes

INGREDIENTS

250 gm spaghetti
250 gm minced beef or lamb
3 tbsp butter
3 tbsp olive oil
1 garlic pod, chopped
1 cup diced mushrooms
1 onion, chopped
1 carrot, shredded
1 tsp flour
1 cup tomato purée
3 fresh tomatoes, blanched and chopped
1 wine glass red wine or a dash of Worcestershire sauce
½ tbsp vinegar
1½ cup stock
salt and pepper to taste
3 tbsp grated cheese

METHOD

1. Heat butter and 2 tbsp olive oil in a pan.
2. Gently fry garlic, mushrooms, onion and carrot.
3. Add minced beef or lamb and cook for 5 minutes, then sprinkle flour over it and mix well.
4. Add tomato purée and cook. Now add blanched tomatoes, wine or Worcestershire sauce, vinegar, stock, salt and pepper, and mix.
5. Simmer till the sauce thickens. Keep aside.
6. Boil the spaghetti with 4 cups of water and salt till it turns soft. Drain and rinse under cold running water.
7. Toss the spaghetti in ground black pepper and olive oil.
8. Place the cooked spaghetti on a platter.
9. Pour the sauce on top and garnish with grated cheese.

Spaghetti with Tomato and Red Pepper Sauce

Serves: 5-6
Time required: 35 minutes

INGREDIENTS

500 gm spaghetti
2 tbsp oil
1 garlic pod, finely chopped
1 onion, sliced
1-inch stick cinnamon
3 bay leaves
5-6 tomatoes, blanched, skinned and finely chopped
1 red bell pepper, sliced
2 tbsp chopped parsley
1 cup tomato purée
1½ cups stock or water
salt and pepper to taste
3 tbsp cheese (preferably Parmesan or Gruyère)
1 tbsp fresh parsley leaves, finely chopped

METHOD

1. Heat oil and add garlic, onion, cinnamon and bay leaves.
2. Now add tomatoes, red bell pepper, ½ tbsp parsley and tomato purée.
3. Cook together for 5 minutes. Remove the bay leaves.
4. To make the sauce, add stock or water and simmer for 5 minutes. Add salt and pepper.
5. Cook the spaghetti separately in 6 cups of water with a pinch of salt. Drain and rinse under cold running water. Place in a large dish.
6. Pour the sauce over the spaghetti and sprinkle grated cheese over it.
7. Garnish with fresh parsley leaves. Serve hot with green salad.

Pesto (Spaghetti Sauce)

Serves: 3-4
Time required: 25 minutes

INGREDIENTS

250 gm spaghetti
1 cup fresh basil
½ cup pine nut or walnut
2 garlic pods, minced
¾ cup grated cheese
6 tbsp olive oil
salt to taste
3 tbsp butter

METHOD

1. Place the basil in a blender. Blend well together with pine nuts or walnuts and garlic, then add cheese.
2. In a shallow pan, add olive oil and the blended mixture and cook slowly over a low flame. Add salt. Keep the sauce aside.
3. Boil the spaghetti separately in 4 cups of water with a pinch of salt. When it is cooked, drain, rinse under cold water and pour into the dish. Add butter and mix well.
4. Serve the sauce separately along with a salad on the side.

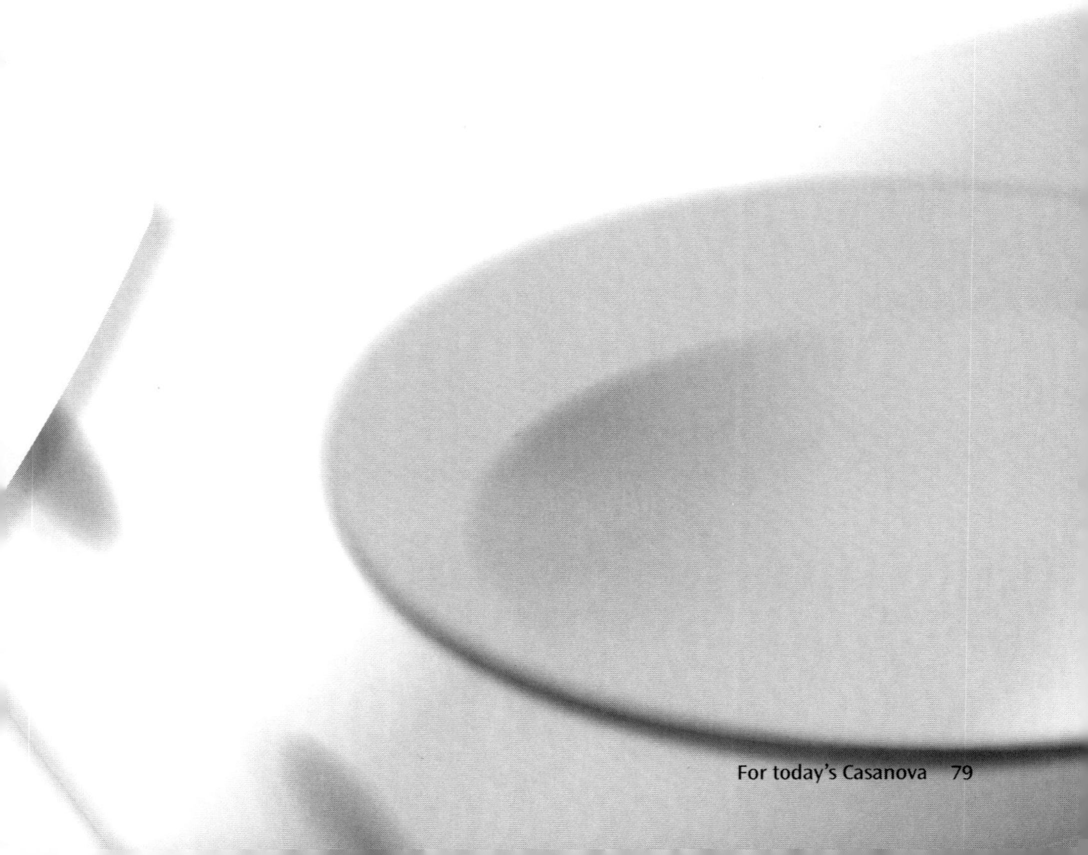

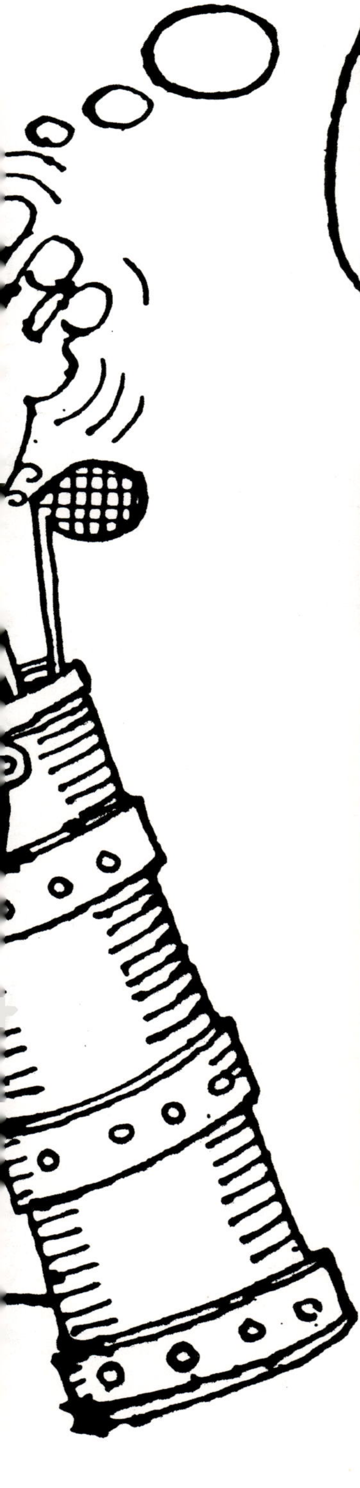

For the golfers

(Round-shaped delights)

Golfers are of varied kinds,
But all have balls on their minds.
They love to birdie, swing and eagle,
And hate anyone to breathe or giggle!
While they take their stance, so called,
That yet another shot may be balled.
We offer them dishes, round in shape,
To look like golf balls, on their plate!
Koftas, meatballs and pork rounds,
Shaped like golf balls but edibly sound!

Italian Meatballs

Serves: 6-8
Time required: 40 minutes

INGREDIENTS

750 gm ground beef/pork
3 slices dark bread, finely torn
2 eggs
1 large onion, chopped
1 tsp salt
4 tbsp olive oil
2 cups tomato purée
½ tsp garlic powder
¾ tsp basil, finely chopped
½ tsp oregano
1 tsp sugar
salt and pepper to taste

METHOD (for the meatballs)

1. Put the bread meat, eggs onion and salt in a blender and blend for a few minutes.
2. Now shape the mixture into balls and brown lightly in 2 tbsp olive oil. Drain and keep aside.

For the sauce:

3. Save the drippings from the browned meatballs. Add tomato purée, garlic powder, basil, oregano, sugar, salt and pepper.
4. Add 2 tbsp olive oil and mix well. Now put in the meatballs and let them cook in the sauce for a while.

Beef/Pork Meatballs

Serves: 5-6
Time required: 20 minutes

INGREDIENTS

500 gm ground beef/pork
¼ cup bread crumbs
2 tbsp chopped parsley
2 tbsp milk
1 egg, beaten
3 tbsp grated Parmesan cheese
1 tsp salt
1 tsp pepper
olive oil or butter to fry

METHOD

1. Mix thoroughly the beef or pork with bread crumbs, parsley, milk, egg and cheese, kneading all the while. Add salt and pepper.
2. Shape the mixture into tiny meatballs.
3. Heat olive oil or butter. Fry the meatballs till brown.

Swedish Meatballs

Serves: 5-6
Time required: 35 minutes

INGREDIENTS

500 gm ground beef
1 egg
1 potato, grated
1 tsp sugar
2 tbsp bread crumbs
2 tbsp sweet cream
½ tsp pepper
½ tsp fresh grated ginger
1 tsp salt
butter to fry

For the sauce

¾ cup butter
1 cup flour
2 glasses milk
salt to taste
1 onion, sliced

METHOD

1. Blend all the ingredients (except butter) to a smooth paste and shape into small balls.
2. Fry in butter, browning well on all sides. Keep aside.

For the sauce:

3. Heat butter and add a little flour and milk to prepare the sauce. Season with salt. Let the meatballs cook in the sauce.
4. If onion flavour is desired, sauté the onion in the drippings before putting in the meatballs.

The Original Meatballs

Serves: 4-5
Time required: 20 minutes

INGREDIENTS

500 gm beef/lamb, ground
¼ tsp pepper
1 tsp salt
¾-1 cup milk
1 onion, grated
1 egg
⅓ cup flour
oil to fry

METHOD

1. Place the extra fine ground beef or lamb mince onto a bowl and add pepper and salt.
2. Now add milk gradually, while kneading continuously. Then knead in the grated onion.
3. Make golf-ball sized meatballs.
4. Dip the meatballs in lightly beaten egg, then brush lightly with flour and deep fry. The meatballs can be served as a snack. Otherwise, add to chicken/vegetable soup.

Meatball Chinois

Serves: 5-6
Time required: 30 minutes

INGREDIENTS

For the meatballs

500 gm pork, ground
¼ cup chopped water chestnuts
2 green onions, chopped
1 egg, beaten
½ cup dry bread crumbs
1 tsp salt
oil to fry

For the sauce

¼ cup cider vinegar
½ cup pineapple syrup
¼ cup brown sugar
½ cup broth
1 tbsp soy sauce
¼-inch ginger, ground
¼ cup sugar
1½ tbsp corn flour
¼ cup water
1 can pineapple chunks, drained

METHOD (for the meatballs)

1. Combine all the ingredients (except oil) and knead well together.
2. Form into medium-sized balls.
3. Fry in hot oil till brown.
4. Drain and keep aside.

For the sauce:

5. Combine vinegar, pineapple syrup, brown sugar, broth, soy sauce, ginger and sugar in a pan.
6. Put the pan on fire. Stir the ingredients till the sugar dissolves.
7. Mix corn flour and water. Stir into the sauce mixture.
8. Cook for about 5 minutes, stirring till the mixture starts to thicken.
9. Now add the meatballs and chunks of pineapple and simmer for 1 minute.

Indian Meatball Curry

Serves: 6-8
Time required: 40 minutes

INGREDIENTS

For the meatballs

500 gm lamb, minced
¼ tsp ground turmeric and coriander
¼ tsp ground *garam masala*
2 garlic pods, crushed
¼-inch ginger, grated
1 tsp red chilly powder
1 large egg
1 tsp salt

For the curry

4 tbsp oil
1 medium-sized onion, finely chopped
1 tomato, finely chopped
2 tsp ginger-garlic paste
½ tsp turmeric powder
1 tsp red chilly powder
¼ tsp ground *garam masala*
½ tsp coriander powder
salt to taste
3 tbsp natural yoghurt
1½ cups water
1 tbsp coriander leaves, finely chopped
1 fresh green chilly, slit lengthwise

METHOD (for the meatballs)

1. Mix all the ingredients listed for the meatball and knead very well. Or, place in a blender and blend till fine.
2. Divide the mixture into small portions and shape them into balls.

For the curry:

3. Heat oil. Fry the onion till golden brown. Add tomatoes, stirring well.
4. Add ginger-garlic paste, turmeric powder, red chilly powder, *garam masala*, coriander powder and salt. Stir well, add yoghurt and mix well. Then add water and bring to a boil.
5. Stir well and leave it to simmer on low heat.
6. Gently place each meatball into the simmering curry, taking care that they do not clump together. Raise the heat till the curry begins to boil. Reduce heat and allow the curry to simmer for about 20 minutes.
7. Garnish with chopped coriander and green chillies.
8. Serve with rice or *roti* (bread).

CHOMP!
CHOMP!
....

For the smilers

(Salads)

There are those who smile a lot
Their teeth, stark white, never rot.
Many are they who would walk a mile,
Just to encounter a dazzling smile!
Do smilers eat? Don't you wonder?
Or would dirty teeth steal their thunder?
A menu for them we'd love to supply
But, to this menu will they comply?
Eat your salads, but eat them raw,
It helps to strengthen a tired jaw.
Chomp, chew and gnash quite heartily
To keep those teeth from getting 'tartar-y'!

Mixed Salad

Serves: 6-8
Time required: 20 minutes

INGREDIENTS

oil to fry
¾ cup croutons
1 cup spinach
1 garlic pod, crushed
2 tbsp mayonnaise
½ tsp mustard paste
salt and pepper to taste
2 cups lettuce, shredded
1 cucumber, chopped
2 tomatoes, chopped
3 cups finely sliced cabbage
½ cup grated cheese

METHOD

1. Deep fry the bread croutons. Drain and keep aside.
2. Wash spinach, cut finely and blanch.
3. Add garlic to the mayonnaise. Stir in mustard paste, salt and pepper to prepare the dressing.
4. Now in a salad bowl, mix together lettuce, cucumber, tomatoes, cabbage and spinach. Add cheese. Toss the dressing over it.
5. Place the croutons on top before serving.

Salad with Honey-Mustard Dressing

Serves: 3-4
Time required: 10 minutes (Chilling time: 30 minutes)

INGREDIENTS

2 green peppers, chopped
1 onion, finely chopped
1 apple, cut into cubes
2-3 baby corns
½ cup shredded cabbage
½ cup tangerine/ orange pieces
¼ cup mayonnaise
1 tbsp French mustard
1 tbsp lemon juice
1 tbsp honey
salt and pepper to taste

METHOD

1. Combine the chopped green peppers, onion, apple, baby corns, cabbage, tangerine/orange pieces and mayonnaise in a salad bowl.
2. Mix together the French mustard, lemon juice, honey, salt and pepper to make the salad dressing.
3. Pour the dressing over the salad ingredients. Chill and serve.

Tomato Aspic Salad

Serves: 6
Time required: 20 minutes (Chilling time: 5-6 hours)

INGREDIENTS

2 cups tomato purée
2 tbsp gelatin
½ cup water
8 whole cloves
1 tsp celery seed
¼ tsp black pepper
4 bay leaves
1 onion, finely chopped
1 tbsp sugar
3 tbsp vinegar
salt to taste
juice of 1 lemon
1 tsp Worcestershire sauce

METHOD

1. Dissolve the gelatin in ½ cup water. Keep aside.
2. Cook together tomato purée, cloves, celery seeds, black pepper, bay leaves, onion, sugar and vinegar on a low fire.
3. Remove from heat. Pass the stewed purée through a coarse strainer to discard the whole spices.
4. Adjust the seasoning and then add the lemon juice, Worcestershire sauce and the dissolved gelatin.
5. Pour this mixture into round-shaped moulds and refrigerate.
6. Serve chilled.

Ripe Mango Salad

Serves: 3-4
Time required: 5 minutes (Chilling time: 20 minutes)

INGREDIENTS

1½ cups ripe mango, cut into cubes
1 tbsp oil
1 small onion, chopped
1 tsp lemon juice
¼ tsp freshly ground black pepper
1 tbsp parsley, finely chopped
salt to taste

METHOD

1. Combine all the above ingredients in a salad bowl. Toss to mix the seasoning.
2. Chill before serving.

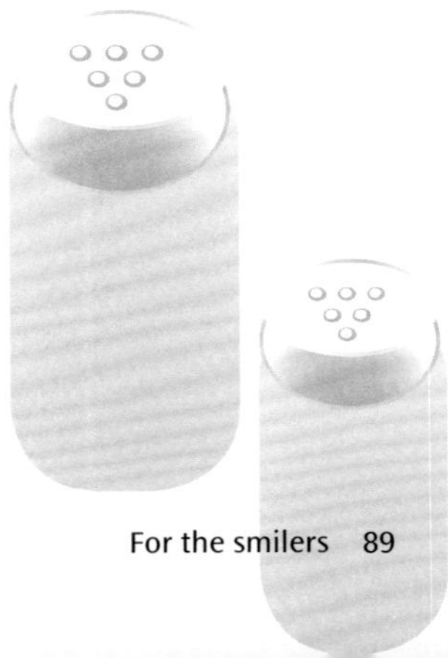

Creamy Potato Salad

Serves: 6-8
Time required: 20 minutes
(Marination time: 2 hours; Chilling time: 30 minutes)

INGREDIENTS

5 medium-sized potatoes
1 medium-sized onion, finely sliced
1 tsp vinegar
salt to taste
½ tsp pepper
1 medium-sized green pepper, diced
¼ cup celery, sliced diagonally
½ small jar of pimento, chopped
½ cup mayonnaise or salad dressing
½ cup sour cream or plain yoghurt
7 lettuce leaves
1 small firm tomato, sliced into wedges

METHOD

1. Boil the potatoes till tender.
2. Drain, peel and cut into cubes.
3. Place the potatoes in a large bowl. Add sliced onions.
4. Pour vinegar, salt and pepper over it and toss until the potatoes are well moistened.
5. Cover and refrigerate for 2 hours until the marinade is absorbed.
6. Now add green pepper, celery and pimento to the potatoes.
7. Combine mayonnaise and sour cream or yoghurt. Pour over the potatoes and toss gently so that they are all well coated.
8. Chill and serve in lettuce lined bowls. Garnish with tomato wedges around the edge.

Chilled Vegetable Salad

Serves: 6-8

Time required: 15 minutes (Chilling time: overnight)

INGREDIENTS

4 large carrots, finely sliced

1 head of cauliflower, separated into florets

1 medium-sized broccoli, separated into florets

3 sweet purple onions, thinly sliced

1 cup fresh mushrooms, (cubed, if large)

20 pitted olives, drained

a few sprigs of fresh dill (optional)

Italian dressing

salt to taste

3-4 lettuce leaves

METHOD

1. Cook the carrots, cauliflower and broccoli till tender.
2. Rinse in ice water to retain their colour.
3. Add sweet purple onions, mushrooms, olives, dill, Italian dressing and salt over it.
4. Refrigerate overnight.
5. Drain and serve in a large salad bowl lined with lettuce leaves.

Waldorf Salad

Serves: 3-4
Time required: 5 minutes (Chilling time: 20 minutes)

INGREDIENTS

4 tbsp mayonnaise
1 tbsp fresh lemon juice
salt to taste
¼ tsp freshly ground pepper
3 red apples, cored and chopped
½ cup celery, thinly sliced
½ cup red seedless grapes, sliced (or ¼ cup raisins)
½ cup chopped and roasted walnuts
3-4 lettuce leaves

METHOD

1. In a medium-sized bowl, whisk together the mayonnaise and fresh lemon juice.
2. Add salt and pepper and mix in the apple, celery, grapes and walnuts.
3. Chill and serve on a bed of fresh lettuce.

Raw Papaya Thai Salad

Serves: 3-4
Time required: 15 minutes

INGREDIENTS

1 medium-sized raw papaya
1½ tbsp lemon juice
salt to taste
1½ tsp light soy sauce
3-4 garlic pods, crushed
2 shredded red chillies
2-3 tsp sugar/ sugarfree sweetner
1 tomato, sliced
2 tbsp crushed and roasted peanuts

METHOD

1. Peel the papaya, grate it, then place it over ice for 15 minutes. Drain and squeeze out the excess moisture.
2. In a glass bowl, mix the grated papaya with lemon juice, salt, soy sauce, garlic, red chillies and sugar or any sugarfree equivalent.
3. Add tomato slices. Garnish with roasted and crushed peanuts.

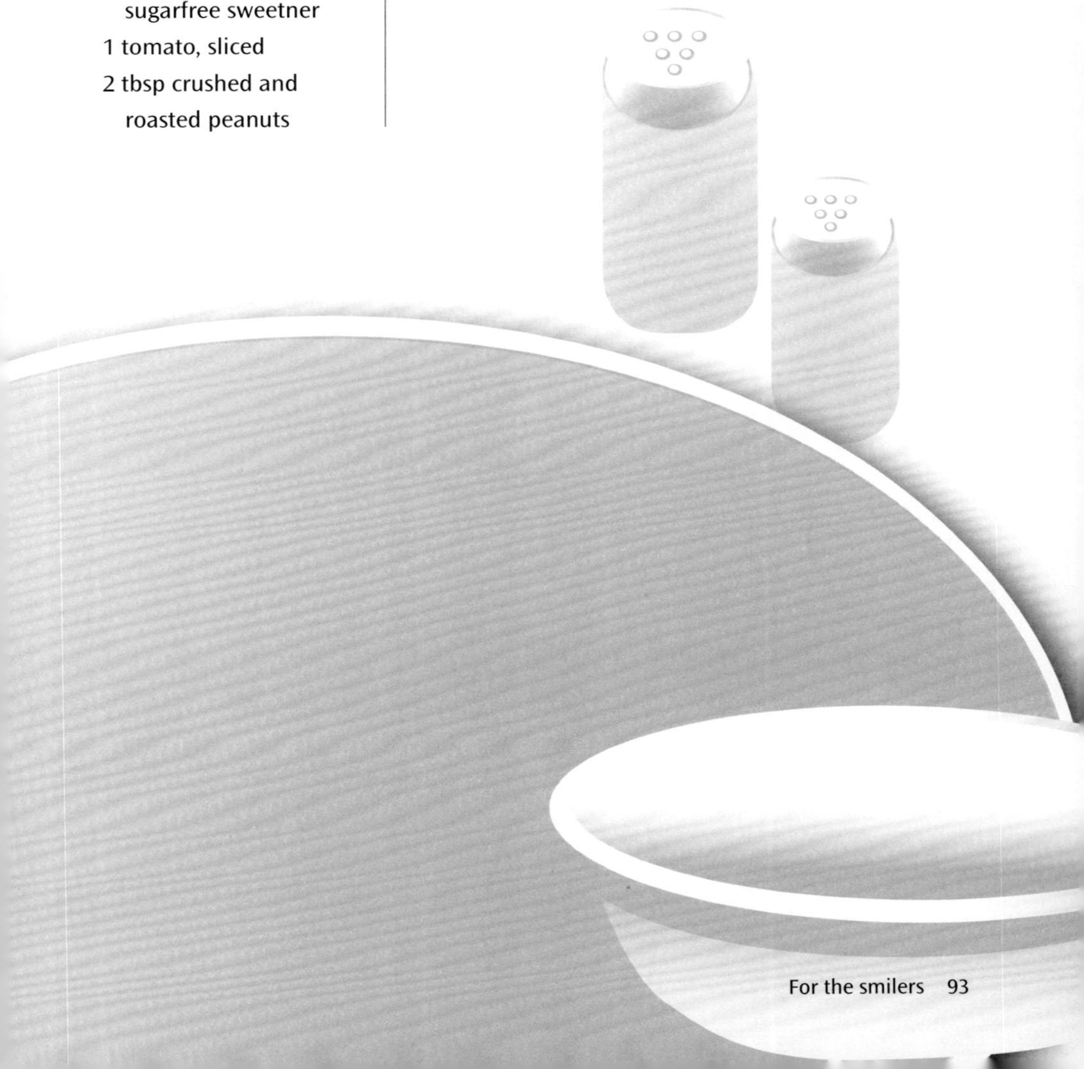

For the bully

(Pork dishes)

For those who love to harangue and bully,
We'll give a menu total and fully.
Since you don't usually express your wishes,
Perhaps we'll offer 'piggy dishes'!
Dumplings, ribs and vindaloo,
Items that will bind porky with you.
Cease, Mr Bully, do simmer down,
Let delicacies of pig wipe your frown!

Pork and Spring Onion Dumplings

Serves: 5-6
Time required: 45 minutes

INGREDIENTS

150 gm pork, minced
1 egg
¾ cup wheat flour
1 tsp oil
3 garlic pods, chopped
2 sprigs coriander leaves, finely chopped
2 spring onions, finely chopped
2 tbsp light soy sauce
salt to taste
1 tsp pepper
4 cups water

METHOD

1. Whisk the egg and mix with the flour.
2. Add oil. Mix and knead a little to form a soft dough. Let the dough rest for about 5 minutes.
3. Blend together minced pork, garlic, coriander, spring onions, soy sauce, salt and pepper.
4. Blend to a fine mixture. Keep aside.
5. Roll out small portions of the dough into small circles (approx. 6-cm diameter).
6. Now place the blended meat filling in the centre. Fold the pastry over and crimp the edges to form a closed dumpling.
7. Boil the water in a pan. Drop the dumplings into the boiling water and cook for 4 minutes. Serve hot.

Spare Ribs Chinois

Serves: 5-6
Time required: 1 hour, 15 minutes (Marination time: 2 hours)

INGREDIENTS

2 racks spare ribs
5 tbsp soy sauce
5 tbsp honey
3 tbsp vinegar
1 tbsp sherry
1 tbsp sugar
1 tsp powdered ginger
1½ cups beef broth
salt to taste
2 garlic pods, minced
2 tbsp oil

METHOD

1. Combine the soy sauce, honey, vinegar, sherry, sugar, ginger, broth, salt, garlic and oil.
2. Marinate the ribs in the mixture for 2 hours.
3. Preheat oven to 170°C.
4. Drain the marinade and roast the ribs for 45-50 minutes. Remove from heat.
5. Pour off the fat, baste with the marinade and grill until brown.
6. Cut into individual ribs and serve immediately.

Vindaloo (Spicy sauce with a dash of vinegar)

Serves: 5-6
Time required: 1 hour (Marination time: 1 hour)

INGREDIENTS

675 gm leg of pork, deboned and cut into 1-inch cubes
1 tsp black peppercorns, freshly ground
3 green chillies, chopped
1½ tsp sugar
8 tbsp malt vinegar
½ tsp turmeric powder
½ tsp cumin seeds
3 tsp coriander seeds
8 green cardamoms
8 red chillies, whole
8 cloves
10 sticks cinnamon (1-inch long)
4 tbsp oil
2-3 potatoes, peeled and cut into cubes
½-inch ginger, chopped
7-8 garlic pods, chopped
2-3 onions, chopped
1.2 litres water
¾ cup pickled onions
salt to taste

METHOD

1. To prepare the marinade, blend thoroughly pepper, green chillies, sugar, malt vinegar, turmeric powder, cumin seeds, coriander seeds, green cardamoms, red chillies, cloves and cinnamon.
2. Rub the marinade over the pork cubes and keep them aside for at least 1 hour.
3. Heat oil in a skillet and deep fry the potatoes until golden brown.
4. Put ginger and garlic in a blender with ½ cup water to make ginger-garlic paste.
5. Transfer oil from skillet to a pan. Heat the oil. Add chopped onions and sauté over medium heat till golden brown. Add ginger-garlic paste and sauté until the oil separates. Then put the pork along with the marinade into the pan and stir for about 2 minutes.
6. Add water (approx. 1.2 litres), bring to a boil, then cover and simmer until the pork is tender.
7. Now put in potatoes and pickled onions. Cook until they are soft. Add salt to taste.

KHEER! KULFI!

For the Krishna conscious

(Indian milk-based desserts)

Hare Ram! Hare Krishan,
For those out on a mission.
The food we offer must be pure,
The aspiring soul to lure!
Bal Krishan, the adorable child—
Prepare his dishes rich, sweet and mild.
Butter, curds and milk he loved,
And all these things shall not be snubbed.
Phirnis, kheer and all milk concoctions,
Cleanse the soul and flush out toxins!
Add shrikhand and kulfi to the lot,
And in consciousness you'll be caught!

Kulfi (Milk-based dessert frozen in moulds)

Serves: 5-6
Time required: 1 hour, 15 minutes (Chilling time: 8-9 hours)

INGREDIENTS

1 litre milk
2 tbsp rice flour
1½ cups sugar
6 tbsp ground almonds
¾ cup double cream, lightly whipped
a few drops of rose water
10-12 unsalted pistachios, cut into slivers

METHOD

1. Pour the milk into a thick-bottomed saucepan and bring to a boil. Reduce heat and simmer uncovered for about 45 minutes until it thickens and reduces to half its quantity. Remove from heat.
2. Pour a little of the thickened milk into a cup. Dissolve rice flour in it and pour it back into the pan. Cook for another 15 minutes over a low flame, stirring continuously until the mixture thickens to a 'pouring-batter' consistency.
3. Add sugar and stir till it dissolves completely. Remove from heat and let it cool completely.
4. Add almonds and whipped cream, rose water and pistachios.
5. Pour the mixture into *kulfi* containers and place in the freezer. The important point to remember with *kulfi* is that you must take it out every hour and whisk thoroughly for the first 3 hours, then leave it to set for 5-6 hours.

Note: *Kulfi* containers are either conical in shape or round and *kulfi* is served in circular slices.

Phirni (Ground rice cooked in flavoured milk)

Serves: 5-6
Time required: 2 hours (Chilling time: 2 hours)

INGREDIENTS

1 litre milk
⅔ cup coarse rice flour
¾ cup sugar
10-12 blanched almonds, cut into slivers
6 cardamoms
1 tsp rose water
10 unsalted pistachios, cut into slivers

METHOD

1. Bring ¾ of the milk to a boil, reduce heat and let it simmer uncovered.
2. Dissolve the rice flour in the rest of the cold milk.
3. Pour mixture into the simmering milk. Stir continuously.
4. Bring the milk to a boil, then reduce heat and simmer for about 1 hour, stirring frequently, until the rice flour is thoroughly cooked and the mixture has thickened to a 'pouring batter' consistency, free of lumps.
5. Add sugar, almonds (retain a few), cardamoms and rose water. Stir well.
6. Cook for a few more minutes until all excess moisture has evaporated and the sugar has completely dissolved.
7. Pour the *phirni* into small individual serving dishes and decorate with pistachios and the rest of the almonds.
8. Serve chilled.

Shrikhand (Dessert of sweetened yoghurt)

Serves: 4-5
Time required: 20 minutes
(Time required for draining yoghurt: 30-40 minutes; Chilling time: 3 hours)

INGREDIENTS

2½ cups yoghurt
10 strands of saffron
4 tbsp warm milk
¾ cup castor sugar
4 green cardamoms, crushed
a pinch of freshly grated nutmeg
5 almonds, chopped
5 pistachios, chopped
9-10 saffron strands

METHOD

1. Drape a square of muslin over a large sieve and put the sieve over a bowl. Pour the yoghurt into the muslin. Let the yoghurt drain for a good 30-40 minutes, by which time most of the whey will drain away.
2. Meanwhile, soak saffron strands in warm milk for about 10 minutes. Place the drained yoghurt in a bowl, add castor sugar and stir continuously to dissolve it completely. Add green cardamoms.
3. Now add saffron milk to the sweetened yoghurt. Stir well to mix. Spoon into small individual serving dishes and leave to chill in the refrigerator.
4. Serve with a sprinkle of nutmeg, almonds and pistachios on top of each dish just before serving.

Kheer (Whole rice cooked in flavoured milk)

Serves: 5-6
Time required: 2 hours

INGREDIENTS

½ cup rice, long grain or *basmati*

1½ litres milk

⅔ cup sugar

10-12 blanched almonds, cut into slivers

15-20 raisins

10-12 unsalted pistachios, cut into slivers

3 green cardamoms, lightly crushed

METHOD

1. Put the rice in a sieve and wash it thoroughly under running cold water until the water runs clear. Drain and place in a thick-bottomed saucepan.
2. Add milk and bring to a boil over medium heat.
3. Reduce heat and stir frequently to prevent the rice from sticking to the bottom.
4. Simmer the pudding until the rice turns soft and mushy and the milk has thickened (the consistency should be that of thick porridge).
5. Add sugar and stir continuously till it dissolves. Add the rest of the ingredients. Stir well and serve hot or cold according to taste.

BORED

For the bored

(Grilled delights)

Tandoori prawns and mixed grill,
For the bored should be a thrill.
Let's get their cells grey or drab,
Livened up and say goodbye to glab!
Every time they have a need,
Let them guzzle some tandoori feed.
And, if the brain threatens to strike
Tell the dullard cells to go take a hike!

Tandoori Prawns

(Clay oven-grilled spicy prawns)

Serves: 5-6
Time required: 30 minutes (Marination time: 1 hour)

INGREDIENTS

12-15 king size prawns, shelled and deveined
8-10 garlic pods, crushed
1-inch ginger, ground
2 tbsp lemon juice
1 tsp salt

For the marinade

½ cup plain yoghurt
¼ cup heavy cream (optional)
2 red onions, finely chopped
¼ tsp turmeric powder
1 tsp chilly powder
½ tsp curry powder
a few drops of red tandoori colouring (optional)

For the garnish

5 lettuce leaves
8 raw onion rings
2 green chillies, finely chopped
4 lemon wedges

METHOD

1. Place the prawns in a shallow dish and marinate with garlic, ginger paste, lemon juice and salt for 10 to 15 minutes. Drain and remove the excess fluid.
2. Mix together ingredients for the marinade for grilling. Pour the marinade over the prawns evenly and refrigerate for 1 hour.
3. Thread the prawns onto a skewer and grill for 3 to 4 minutes on each side or place the prawns on a heat-proof dish and grill under a very hot preheated grill for 12 minutes, turning over once. Alternatively, roast in a moderately hot tandoor for 5-6 minutes or in a charcoal grill for 6-7 minutes.
4. Serve on a bed of lettuce with onion rings, chopped green chillies and lemon wedges.

Kastoori Kebab

(Chicken grilled and roasted with creamy marination of gram flour)

Serves: 5-6
Time required: 30 minutes (Marination time: 1 hour)

INGREDIENTS

12 breasts of chicken
1½-inch ginger, ground
12-15 garlic pods, ground
1 tsp pepper powder
1 tsp salt
¼ cup lemon juice
½ cup butter
2 tsp groundnut oil
½ cup gram flour
¼ cup bread crumbs
½-inch ginger, finely chopped
2 tbsp coriander leaves, finely chopped
½ tsp green cardamom powder

For the batter

3 eggs
½ tsp black cumin seeds
10-12 strands of saffron, soaked in 2 tbsp warm milk

METHOD

1. Clean the chicken, remove the skin, debone and cut each breast into two.
2. Mix ginger, garlic, pepper, salt and lemon juice. Rub this mixture over the chicken pieces. Keep aside for 1 hour.
3. Heat butter and oil in a skillet. Add gram flour and sauté over medium heat until golden brown. Remove about 20 gm of the gram flour and keep aside.
4. Add bread crumbs, ginger, coriander and the marinated chicken. Sauté the chicken for 3-4 minutes.
5. Separate egg yolks, discard the whites, transfer to a bowl, and add cumin, saffron and the gram flour kept aside. Whisk well to prepare the batter.
6. Preheat the oven to 170°C. Skewer 6 chicken pieces together, leaving a gap of 2 inches and then skewer the next lot. Coat each set with the batter and roast in the oven for 8-10 minutes.Alternatively, roast in a moderately hot tandoor for 5-6 minutes or in a charcoal grill for 6-7 minutes.
7. Remove and sprinkle cardamom powder over the kebabs. Serve hot.

Tandoori Chicken

(Clay oven-grilled chicken)

Serves: 5-6
Time required: 40 minutes (Marination time: 4-5 hours)

INGREDIENTS

600 gm chicken
1 tsp red chilly powder
¼ cup lemon juice
1 tsp salt
½ cup yoghurt
½ cup cream
3 tsp ginger paste
3 tsp garlic paste
1 tsp cumin powder
1 tsp *garam masala*
10-12 strands of saffron, soaked in 2 tbsp warm milk
1 drop of orange colouring
butter for basting

METHOD

1. Clean the chicken, remove the skin and make deep incisions—3 on each breast, 3 on each thigh, and 2 on each drumstick.
2. Make a paste with red chilly powder, lemon juice and salt and rub over the chicken evenly. Keep aside for 15 minutes.
3. Whisk yoghurt in a large bowl. Add the remaining ingredients (except butter) and mix well. Rub the chicken with this mixture. Keep aside for 4 hours.
4. Preheat the oven to 170°C. Skewer the chicken pieces, leaving a gap of at least 2 inches between the pieces. Keep a tray underneath to collect the drippings. Grill in oven for 10 minutes.
5. Alternatively, roast the chicken in a moderately hot tandoor for approx. 8 minutes, or in a charcoal grill for about the same time.
6. Remove and hang the skewers to let the excess moisture drip off (approx. 4-5 minutes), baste with butter and roast again for 3-4 minutes.

Tandoori Lobster

(Clay oven-grilled spicy lobster)

Serves: 4

Time required: 30 minutes (Marination time: 2 hours)

INGREDIENTS

4 lobsters (large size)

1 egg

½-inch ginger, finely chopped

¾ cup cream

a pinch of *ajwain* (also known as bishop's weed or carrom seeds)

2 tbsp lemon juice

¼ cup gram flour

2 tbsp *garam masala*

½ tsp white pepper powder

1 tsp salt

butter for basting

METHOD

1. Boil, cool, shell and devein the lobster. (If you wish to serve the lobsters in their shells, cut into half, remove from the shells, then wash the shells and keep aside).
2. Break the egg in a bowl, add ginger and the remaining ingredients (except butter). Whisk and then rub the lobster with this mixture. Keep aside for 2 hours.
3. Preheat the oven to 170°C. Skewer the lobster, from mouth to tail. Keep a tray underneath to collect the drippings. Grill in oven for 12 minutes.
4. Alternatively, roast in a moderately hot tandoor for 8 minutes. If using charcoal fire, grill for the same time.
5. Remove and hang the skewers to allow the excess moisture to drip off (approx. 3 minutes), baste with butter, and roast again for 3 minutes.
6. Before serving, place the lobsters inside the shells.

For lovers: young and old
(Nibbles)

Be the lovers young or old,
They are made from a single mould.
Their steps have a bounce, their eyes twinkle,
They see only beauty and not the wrinkle!
You and I may think them rude.
For forever are they lost in their mood,
Hors d'oeuvres, cocktail snacks and bites,
Take them through their romantic rites!

Pakoras (Vegetarian/non-vegetarian fritters)

Serves: 7-8
Time required: 30 minutes

INGREDIENTS

For the pakora

500 gm mixed vegetables: potatoes, onions, cauliflower, mushrooms, eggplants, etc.,
or 5 boiled eggs, or
200 gm cottage cheese
or 2 chicken breasts
oil to fry

For the batter

2 cups gram flour, sieved
1 tsp *ajwain* seeds (known as bishop's weed or carrom seeds), or thyme
1 tsp *garam masala* powder
2 cups water
salt to taste

Potatoes

Peel and slice into 1.25-cm thick slices. Soak in water until required to avoid discolouration. Drain and pat dry.

Onions

Peel and slice into 1.25-cm thick round slices. Do not separate the layers.

Cauliflower

Cut into 2-inch long florets. If they are too thick, slice lengthwise, otherwise they will remain uncooked.

Mushrooms

Cut into half if too big. Wipe thoroughly.

Eggplants

Slice into ½-inch thick round slices. Soak in cold water until required to avoid discolouration. Drain and pat dry.

Green chillies

For anyone who is brave enough to tackle them—make an incision on one side of the chilly lengthwise. This will prevent it from bursting during frying.

Cottage cheese

Press cottage cheese to drain out excess water. Cut into 1-inch cubes.

Eggs

Hard-boil the eggs. Shell and cut into slices or quarters.

Chicken

Use deboned chicken breast. Cut into small pieces. Marinate for 30 minutes in a little lemon juice, crushed garlic and green chilly. Drain and pat dry before use.

METHOD (for the batter)

1. To prepare the batter, place the gram flour and the remaining dry ingredients in a bowl. Pour water gradually and beat to a smooth batter. The consistency should be that of a thick pancake batter. Leave aside to rest for 10 minutes.
2. Once you have prepared the vegetables/ ingredients of your choice, lightly beat the batter for another minute or so.
3. Heat oil in a deep fryer or wok to smoking point. Now reduce the heat to medium. To test the temperature of the oil, sprinkle a few drops of batter into it. They should rise to the surface almost immediately.
4. Dip a few pieces of the vegetables/other ingredients into the batter to thoroughly coat them. Then using your fingers, lift them out of the batter and drop them gently into the hot oil. The safest way to avoid splashing is by gently lowering the vegetables against the edge of the pan.
5. Do not fry too many at a time. Fry for a few minutes, then carefully turn them over. They may tend to stick together, do not try to separate them now—that can be done after they have been taken out of the hot oil.
6. Fry for 3-5 minutes till golden on both sides. Then lift and drain thoroughly against the side of the pan. Place them on absorbent paper for a few minutes to drain any excess oil. Transfer to a serving dish and serve hot.

Marinated Prawns

Serves: 5-6
Time required: 20 minutes (Chilling time: 1 hour)

INGREDIENTS

700 gm fresh or frozen uncooked jumbo prawns, in their shell
½-inch stick celery, washed and trimmed
1 bay leaf
6 black peppercorns
2 tsp salt
1½ tbsp olive oil
4 tbsp lemon juice
2 sprigs fresh dill, finely chopped
3 tbsp vinegar

METHOD

1. Shell the prawns, leaving the tails on. Put them in a large saucepan of boiling water with celery, bay leaf, peppercorns and salt. Simmer for 3 minutes and then drain well. Discard the whole spices.
2. Mix lemon juice, 1 tsp dill, vinegar and oil in a bowl and toss the prawns in it. Chill.
3. To serve, drain the prawns well and discard the flavourings. Garnish with 1 tsp fresh dill.

Party Prawns

Prepare as above, but double the quantity. Spoon into crystalline ice bowls and serve with cocktail sticks.

Spring Onion Dip

Time required: 10 minutes (Chilling time: 30 minutes)

INGREDIENTS

4 tbsp thinly sliced spring onions
1 cup sour cream
1 tsp instant beef stock powder
1 tsp Worcestershire sauce
salt to taste

METHOD

1. Mix all the ingredients together in a small bowl. Cover and chill.
2. Serve either with raw vegetable sticks or potato crisps or chips.

Chinese Chicken Wings

Serves: 6-8
Time required: 50 minutes

INGREDIENTS

750 gm chicken wings
1 tbsp oil
2 spring onions,
cut into 3-inch pieces
1 cup soy sauce
½ cup dry sherry
3 tbsp tomato ketchup
1 tbsp sugar
salt to taste
½-inch ginger, ground
2 tbsp lettuce, shredded
(optional)

METHOD

1. Cut off the chicken wing tips at the joint and discard, then cut each wing in half at the joint.
2. Heat oil in a large saucepan.
3. Put in the chicken wings and two-thirds of the spring onions. Fry for about 5-6 minutes.
4. Reduce heat and add the rest of the cut spring onions, soy sauce, sherry, tomato ketchup, sugar, salt and ground ginger. Stir well. Cover and cook for 25 minutes, stirring occasionally.
5. Remove the lid and cook a further 10 minutes, stirring frequently, until almost all the liquid is absorbed and the chicken wings are tender.
6. Serve hot or cold on a bed of shredded lettuce.

Guacamole Dip

Time required: 20 minutes

INGREDIENTS

2 avocados, peeled and
cut into half
2 tbsp lemon juice
1¼ tsp salt
1 tomato,
skinned and chopped
½ small onion,
finely chopped
1 garlic pod, crushed
½ tsp chilly powder
1 tbsp cilantro/coriander,
finely chopped

METHOD

1. Mash the avocado with lemon juice and stir in salt, chopped tomato, onion, garlic and chilly powder to taste.
2. Spoon into a bowl. Garnish with coriander if you wish.
3. Serve with potato crisps, tacos or any other chips.

Peppery Mayonnaise Dip

Time required: 20 minutes (Chilling time: 30 minutes)

INGREDIENTS

1 cup mayonnaise
1 onion, grated
2 tsp tarragon vinegar
2 tsp chopped chives
2 tsp mild chilly sauce
½ tsp curry powder
¼ tsp pepper
½ tsp salt

METHOD

1. Mix together all the ingredients. Cover and chill.
2. Spoon the mixture into a bowl.
3. Place the bowl in the centre of a plate and surround with raw vegetables like carrot sticks, cucumber, horseradish sticks, steamed cauliflower florets, etc., that have been peeled and cut into sticks.

Yoghurt and Cream Cheese Dip

Time required: 20 minutes (Chilling time: 30 minutes)

INGREDIENTS

1 cup cream cheese, softened
¾ cup plain yoghurt
a pinch of dried dill
¾ tsp salt

METHOD

1. Beat the cream cheese until smooth and fluffy.
2. Gradually beat in the remaining ingredients until all are well mixed.
3. Pour in a small bowl, cover and chill.
4. Serve with either raw vegetable sticks or potato crisps.

DEEVINE! ...

For the toothless
(Soft puddings)

Dentures may come and dentures may go
We offer soufflés and sweet puddings!
Soft and delicious and very tempting
Are features of these special puddings
Try them with a scoop of fresh cream
Let cholesterol levels go beserk and scream
Custards and puddings at all times you'll see
Right from the days spent on Granny's knee!

Bread Pudding

Serves: 6
Time required: 1 hour

INGREDIENTS

8 slices of white bread
1 tbsp butter
3 eggs
3 egg yolks
2 tbsp sugar or
½ cup maple syrup
1 cup heavy cream
1 cup milk
2 tsp vanilla essence
10-12 almonds,
blanched and slivered
25-30 soaked raisins
½ tsp grated nutmeg

METHOD

1. Preheat oven to 170°C.
2. Grease the baking dish with butter.
3. Cut the bread slices into 1-inch squares. Fill the baking dish with bread.
4. Whisk together eggs and egg yolks. Add sugar/maple syrup, cream, milk and vanilla essence.
5. Pour the egg mixture over the bread. Push the bread down into the egg mixture to moisten it.
6. Place almonds and raisins on top and sprinkle with grated nutmeg.
7. Place the baking dish in the oven. Bake for 45 minutes or until lightly browned. Serve warm.

Lemon Soufflé

Serves: 6
Time required: 1 hour

INGREDIENTS

4 eggs
⅓ cup sugar
juice and rind
of 1 lemon

METHOD

1. Set the oven at 170°C.
2. Separate eggs and the yolks.
3. Beat the egg whites till stiff.
4. Add the entire sugar gradually spoon by spoon, while beating the egg whites.
5. Without washing the beater, beat the yolks in another bowl till creamy.
6. Add the grated rind and juice of lemon.
7. Fold in the egg whites and pour into baking dish.
8. Bake for 40 minutes. Serve warm.

Shahi Tukda

(Fried bread slices soaked in sweetened cream)

Serves: 6-8
Time required: 25 minutes (Chilling time: 2 hours)

INGREDIENTS

10 bread slices
3 tbsp butter/clarified butter
2 cups milk
10-12 strands of saffron, soaked in 2 tbsp warm milk
1¼ cup sugar
3-4 drops vanilla essence
1 cup full cream
½ cup condensed milk
10-15 pistachios, almonds and cashew nuts, finely chopped

METHOD

1. Cut the bread slices in triangles or squares.
2. Heat butter or clarified butter in a deep frying pan.
3. Fry the bread pieces till golden brown. Drain the excess butter and keep aside.
4. Boil the milk. Add saffron strands, sugar, vanilla essence, cream and condensed milk to it.
5. In a shallow bowl, place the fried bread pieces and pour the sweetened milk over it.
6. Let the bread soak up the milk.
7. Garnish with pistachios, almonds and cashew nuts.
8. Serve chilled.

Soft Custard

Serves: 6
Time required: 20 minutes (Chilling time: 2 hours)

INGREDIENTS

6 yolks or 3 eggs
¼ cup white/brown sugar
⅛ tsp salt
2 cups scalded milk
1 tsp vanilla essence or sherry

METHOD

1. Beat the yolks or whole eggs and blend well.
2. Add sugar, salt and milk.
3. Cook and stir over low heat until the custard thickens and coats the spoon (approx. 7 minutes).
4. Flavour the custard with vanilla essence or sherry.
5. Chill and serve.

For the workaholics

(Quickies)

Who gives himself B.P., and others colic?
The demented, masochistic workaholic!
He thrives on work, both day and night,
And never has time for his appetite.
Strange it may seem, but human he is
Though he runs around in an endless tizz!
For him we have dishes called 'quickies'
That can be made in just two jiffies!
Though his values he does indeed confuse,
Yet to his system some nutrients we'll infuse.
Eat these 'quickies'—hearty or light,
Then work all day and work all night!

Hearty Tuna Salad

Serves: 6
Time required: 20 minutes (Chilling time: 1 hour)

INGREDIENTS

1 tin tuna, flaked (but firm)
½ cup French beans, cut into ½-inch pieces
¾ cup thinly sliced celery
½ cup mayonnaise
1 tbsp lemon juice
1 tsp soy sauce
a pinch of garlic powder
salt to taste
¾ cup crisp potato wafers
3-4 lettuce leaves

METHOD

1. Steam the French beans till soft but crisp.
2. Combine flaked tuna, beans, celery, mayonnaise, lemon juice, soy sauce, garlic powder and salt.
3. Mix well and chill.
4. Just before serving, crush potato wafers and add. Toss lightly.
5. Serve on a bed of lettuce leaves.

He-Man Potato Salad

Serves: 5
Time required: 25 minutes

INGREDIENTS

4 cups cooked, boiled and sliced potatoes
4 slices bacon
2 tbsp oil
2 onions, chopped
¼ cup chopped celery
2 tbsp flour
4 tbsp vinegar
1 cup water
a pinch of black pepper
1 tsp sugar
salt to taste

METHOD

1. In a skillet heat oil and fry the bacon till crisp. Remove and crumble.
2. Drain excess oil from the skillet, retaining only a little of the drippings.
3. Stir fry onion and celery and keep aside.
4. In the same skillet, stir in the flour. Add water and vinegar. Cook till the flour thickens.
5. Add the bacon and all the remaining ingredients including the potatoes.
6. Stir and mix well and continue heating for 5 minutes. Serve when cooled.

Sesame Chicken on the Run

Serves: 4
Time required: 30 minutes

INGREDIENTS

4 chicken breasts, deboned
2 tsp sesame seeds
½ cup flour
1 tsp salt
¼ tsp pepper
1 egg
1 tbsp milk
shortening or oil to fry

METHOD

1. Mix together the sesame seeds, flour, salt and pepper.
2. In a separate bowl, whisk the egg and add milk to it.
3. Now dip the chicken pieces in the egg/milk mixture, then dust with the flour.
4. Fry in hot oil till tender on the inside and crisp on the outside. Serve with green salad.

Chicken on Sticks

Serves: 6
Time required: 40 minutes (Marination time: 15-20 minutes)

INGREDIENTS

500 gm boneless chicken, cut into long thin strips
1 tsp salt
1 tbsp vinegar
2-3 tsp chilly paste
1 tsp soy sauce
1 tsp red chilly powder
1 tbsp tomato sauce
oil to fry

METHOD

1. Place the boneless chicken strips in a bowl. Add salt and vinegar.
2. Allow the chicken to stand for 15-20 minutes.
3. Drain the chicken well. Pat dry. Return to the bowl.
4. Add all the remaining ingredients except oil. Skewer each piece of chicken onto a toothpick. Set aside.
5. Heat oil in a pan. Place a few chicken pieces on it. Cook on all sides.
6. Remove the cooked chicken and repeat the process with the remaining lot. Serve hot with green *chutney* or ketchup.

Note: You can prepare beforehand and freeze, then microwave and serve when in a hurry.

Puffy Omelette

Serves: 1
Time required: 20 minutes

INGREDIENTS

3 eggs
¼ tsp salt
3 tbsp water
2-3 tbsp butter or oil

METHOD

1. Separate the egg whites from the yolks.
2. Whisk the yolks. Add salt and water. Beat till fluffy.
3. Now add the stiffly beaten egg whites. Fold into the yolk mixture.
4. Heat the skillet and put oil or butter.
5. Pour in the egg mixture and cook till it is brown on the underneath.
6. Place in a preheated oven at 140°C and brown the top. Serve immediately.

Garlic Prawns

Serves: 7-8
Time required: 15 minutes (Marination time: 1 hour)

INGREDIENTS

30 tiger prawns, peeled and deveined
½ cup olive oil
1 tbsp Dijon mustard
3 garlic pods, minced
juice of 1 lemon
juice of 1 orange
1 tsp dried basil
2 tbsp white wine (optional)
salt to taste

METHOD

1. In a glass dish, mix together the olive oil, Dijon mustard, minced garlic, lemon juice, orange juice, dried basil, white wine and salt.
2. Add the prawns. Stir to coat with the mixture. Cover and marinate for 1 hour.
3. Heat an outdoor grill to high heat.
4. Thread the prawns onto skewers.
5. Grill for 3-5 minutes, turning once until pink.

Spanish Rice

Serves: 6
Time required: 40 minutes

INGREDIENTS

½ cup rice (any long grain rice or *basmati*)
1 tbsp oil
2 slices bacon, cut fine
1 onion, chopped
4-5 tomatoes, chopped
1 tsp salt
¼ tsp cracked black peppercorns
1 bay leaf
1 cup boiling water

METHOD

1. Heat oil in a pan. Fry the bacon till crisp and keep aside.
2. Add onions and cook till golden.
3. Add the uncooked rice. Cook for 5 minutes, stirring constantly.
4. Put in chopped tomatoes, salt, peppercorns and bay leaf. Add water.
5. Bake in a greased baking dish for 20 minutes in a preheated oven at 150°C.
6. Serve hot.

Jingle
Jingle

For the intelligent

(Food for grey cells)

Tabouleh, hummus and patties
Suit to a tee the intelligent veneer!
Something to think about and ponder,
Set the grey cells agog and a wonder.
Serve them paté made of brinjal,
And watch those grey cells go a jingle!

Aubergine Paté

Serves: 8
Time required: 20 minutes

INGREDIENTS

1 large aubergine or eggplant
1 tbsp oil
1 onion, chopped
4 garlic pods, crushed
a pinch of red chilly powder
4 cups yoghurt
½ cup coconut milk
1 tsp coriander powder
1 tsp cumin powder
salt to taste
juice of 1 lemon

METHOD

1. Roast the entire eggplant over flame, turning it over so that it is evenly browned and soft.
2. Peel and mash.
3. Fry onion and garlic. Now add the mashed aubergine paste and sauté till cooked.
4. Add red chilly powder, yoghurt and coconut milk.
5. Mix in coriander powder, cumin powder and salt.
6. Remove from heat. When paste has cooled, add lemon juice.

Hummus

Serves: 6
Time required: 20 minutes (Soaking time: overnight)

INGREDIENTS

2 cups Garbanzo beans or *kabuli channa* (soaked overnight and boiled with a little cooking soda)
5 garlic pods, crushed
salt to taste
5-6 tbsp tahini (paste of sesame seed)
juice of 5-6 lemons
few drops of olive oil
a few olives
2-3 red chillies

METHOD

1. Blend the boiled beans into a paste. Add a little water.
2. Add salt and tahini to garlic and mix well.
3. Pour in the lemon juice.
4. Now add the beans paste.
5. Transfer the mixture to a serving bowl. Stir in a few drops of olive oil. Garnish with olives and red chillies.

Cottage Cheese Patties

Serves: 4
Time required: 25 minutes

INGREDIENTS

250 gm cottage cheese
½ cup semolina
½ tbsp oil or clarified butter
a pinch of *garam masala*
2-4 green chillies, chopped
1¾ cup milk
salt to taste
1 cup white flour
1 cup bread crumbs
oil to fry

METHOD

1. Brown the semolina in oil or clarified butter in a pan.
2. Add *garam masala* and green chillies.
3. Crush the cottage cheese by hand and add to the pan. Now pour in the milk and salt and let the mixture thicken.
4. Remove from fire and let the mixture cool. Then shape the mixture into patties.
5. Coat each patty with the flour.
6. Roll over bread crumbs and shallow fry in oil.
7. Serve hot with vegetables or salad.

Tabouleh

Serves: 3
Time required: 20 minutes

INGREDIENTS

⅔ cup bulgur wheat
2 onions, finely chopped
2 tomatoes, chopped
1tbsp chopped watercress (optional)
½ tbsp chopped celery (optional)
1 tbsp chopped parsley
1 tbsp chopped mint
salt to taste
4 tbsp olive oil
5 tbsp lemon juice

METHOD

1. Soak bulgur wheat in cold water for a while. Drain well.
2. Add onions, tomatoes, watercress, celery, parsley, mint and salt to bulgur wheat.
3. Mix everything together and toss in olive oil and lemon juice.
4. Serve with pita bread.

For the motivated

(Bird food)

There are food lovers with lots of style,
You can spot them from many a mile!
These 'motivated few' try their best,
With rare combinations that excell the test.
Turkey and duck for supper go well,
With sauces, dressings and trimmings swell.
Have a change from the usual rooster and hen
Try these 'birds' that go well for special men!

Shanghai Duck

Serves: 6-8
Time required: 2 hours

INGREDIENTS

2 kg oven-ready duck
8 medium leeks
1 cup dry sherry
1 cup soy sauce
3 tsp sugar
½-inch root ginger, peeled or 1¼ tsp ginger paste
2 glasses water
salt to taste
3 small carrots, cut into strips

METHOD

1. Prepare the leeks. Trim the roots, discard the tough outer leaves and cut about 15 cm from the thick white root section. Rinse thoroughly under running water and drain. Cover and refrigerate. Cut the remaining leaves across into 1-cm slices and wash. Put them into a saucepan large enough to hold the duck.
2. Remove the giblets from the duck. Trim as much fatty skin as possible from around the neck and body cavity of the duck. Rinse the duck and giblets well and pat dry with kitchen paper towel.
3. Place the duck, breast side down, over the leeks in the pan and tuck the giblets around it.
4. Add the sherry, soy sauce, sugar, ginger, water and salt to the pan. Bring to a boil, reduce the heat, cover and simmer for about 30 minutes.
5. Carefully turn the duck over, cover and cook for a further hour, basting occasionally with the cooking liquid.
6. Skim the fat from the cooking liquid and discard. Then arrange the carrots and the leeks, kept in the refrigerator around the duck and bring to a boil. Cover and simmer for a further 20 minutes.
7. Baste occasionally during cooking, until the duck and vegetables are tender when tested with a fork or skewer. Skim any fat from the sauce. Serve immediately.

Duck à l'Orange

Serves: 6-8
Time required: 2-3 hours

INGREDIENTS

2 kg oven-ready duck
1 knob of butter
salt and pepper to taste
¾ cup white wine
1 tbsp sugar
1 tbsp vinegar
2 tbsp brandy
juice of 3 oranges, preferably tangerines
juice of 1 lemon
rind of 1 orange, finely shredded
2 tsp corn flour
½ cup water

For the garnish

1 orange, sliced
1 bunch watercress, trimmed

METHOD

1. Rub the breast of the duck with the butter and sprinkle salt and pepper over it. Pour the wine over it and place the duck in a roasting tin and cook in a preheated oven at 170°C for 1½ hours, basting occasionally.
2. Dissolve the sugar in a pan with the vinegar and heat until it caramelises. Add brandy, orange and lemon juices and simmer gently for 5 minutes.
3. When the duck is cooked, remove it from the roasting tin, cut it and place the pieces on a heated serving dish. Keep hot.
4. Spoon the excess fat from the roasting tin and add the shredded rind and the orange sauce to the sediment and juices remaining in the tin. Blend the corn flour with water, stir it into the juices and return the tin to the heat. Bring to a boil and cook for 2-3 minutes, stirring continuously. Season.
5. Pour the sauce over the duck joints and garnish with orange slices and watercress.

Turkey à la King

Serves: 6
Time required: 20 minutes

INGREDIENTS

400 gm cooked turkey
3 tbsp butter/margarine
1 cup mushrooms, sliced
½-1 red or green bell pepper
2 tbsp chicken fat (optional)
1½ tbsp flour
1 cup milk/chicken stock
1 egg
2-3 tbsp thin cream
salt to taste
1 tbsp chopped parsley

METHOD

1. Heat 1 tbsp butter in a pan. Add mushrooms and bell pepper and cook gently until tender.
2. In another pan, melt 2 tbsp butter or chicken fat. Blend flour in milk or chicken stock separately and pour into the pan and cook on low heat.
3. When the sauce has thickened, add the egg and cream blended well together. Simmer for 2-3 minutes. Season well.
4. Add the cooked turkey, mushrooms and sliced bell pepper and heat together for a few minutes.
5. Garnish with chopped parsley and serve on hot buttered toast.

Turkey Croquettes

Serves: 4
Time required: 30 minutes

INGREDIENTS

300 gm turkey, minced and cooked
2 tbsp butter/margarine
2 tbsp flour
1 glass milk/chicken stock
salt and pepper to taste
1 egg, whisked
1 cup bread crumbs
oil to fry

METHOD

1. In a pan, melt butter. Add flour blended with milk or chicken stock and season well.
2. Make a thick sauce. Add the turkey, mix well and allow the mixture to cool slightly.
3. Form the mixture into croquette shapes. Dip each croquette into the egg and roll over the bread crumbs.
4. Fry in oil until crisp and golden brown on either side.

Turkey Cordon Bleu

Serves: 6
Time required: 1 hour

INGREDIENTS

6 slices turkey breast
6 slices Gruyère or Cheddar cheese
6 slices ham, cooked
1 tbsp plain flour
1 tsp paprika
5-6 tbsp butter
½ cup dry white wine
1 chicken stock cube, crumbled
1 tbsp corn flour
½ cup double or whipped cream
salt to taste

METHOD

1. Beat out the turkey slices, place a slice of cheese, then a slice of ham over each one, folding in the edges. Fold the slices in half, securing the edges with wooden cocktail sticks.
2. Mix the flour and paprika and coat the turkey parcels.
3. Melt the butter in a large pan, add the turkey parcels and fry gently for 10 minutes until brown all over.
4. Add the wine and stock cube. Reduce heat, cover the pan and simmer gently for 30 minutes.
5. Remove the turkey parcels to a warmed serving dish. Take out the wooden cocktail sticks.
6. Mix the corn flour and cream until smooth and gradually stir into the liquid in the pan. Cook gently until it thickens. Add salt. Now pour the sauce over the turkey parcels.

SHARES
RACING BETS
LOTTERY

For those almost there but not quite

(Rice dishes)

For the almost there but not quite
Who lose heart with victory in sight
For those who try and try their best
But somehow just cannot reach the crest.
For those who fret and worry and fidget
And lose the lottery by just one digit!
For those who panic and sell their stocks
Before bonus and rights are added to the lots.
For them we recommend dishes of rice—
Aromatic, spicy and very nice!

Nine Gems Rice

Serves: 4-5
Time required: 40 minutes (Soaking time: 30 minutes)

INGREDIENTS

2½ cups *basmati* rice
2 tbsp clarified butter
1 tsp black cumin seeds
1 medium onion, finely sliced
4 green cardamoms
4 cloves
1-inch stick cinnamon
2 bay leaves
8 whole black peppercorns
2 cups assorted fresh or frozen vegetables (cauliflower, carrots, peas, mushrooms, French beans, turnips, tomatoes, okra) cut into small equal-sized pieces
2 tsp salt
1 tsp chilly powder
water

METHOD

1. Put the rice in a sieve and wash it thoroughly under running cold water till it runs clear. Soak in plenty of cold water for 30 minutes. Drain the rice in a sieve and let it stand for a minute or two.
2. Heat clarified butter in a large heavy-bottomed saucepan. Add the black cumin seeds and let it splutter. Now add the onion and stir fry for 3-5 minutes to a rich golden colour. Add the green cardamoms, cloves, cinnamon, bay leaves and black peppercorns and continue frying for another few seconds.
3. Add the vegetables, salt and chilly powder. Stir fry for another 1-2 minutes, then reduce heat, cover and allow it to stew for 5 minutes.
4. Add the rice to the pan, stir gently to mix all the ingredients (do not stir too hard or the rice grains will break). Level the rice with a spatula, add enough water to cover the rice by about 1 inch. Bring to a boil, then reduce the heat. Cover and cook undisturbed for about 20 minutes or until the water has been absorbed completely and the grains are separate.
5. Gently fork the rice, gradually working down to the bottom. Cover for some time. Serve hot.

Spicy Coconut Rice

Serves: 4-5
Time required: 40 minutes (Soaking time: 30 minutes)

INGREDIENTS

2½ cups *basmati* rice
2 tbsp clarified butter
2 tsp black mustard seeds
¼ cup coconut, freshly grated
salt to taste
water

METHOD

1. Put the rice in a sieve and wash it thoroughly under running cold water till it runs clear. Soak in plenty of cold water for 30 minutes. Drain the rice in a sieve and let it stand for a minute or two.
2. Heat clarified butter in a large heavy-bottomed saucepan. Add mustard seeds and as soon as they begin to splutter, add half of the coconut. Fry the coconut, stirring constantly until it just begins to change colour.
3. Add the drained rice and salt to the coconut and stir fry for 1 minute. Level the rice with a spatula and pour in enough water to cover the rice by about 1 inch. Bring to a boil, reduce heat, and cover the pan with a tight-fitting lid. Cook for about 20 minutes until the rice is tender and all the moisture is absorbed.
4. Dry roast the remaining coconut under a hot grill or in a frying pan for a few minutes until it turns a pale golden colour.
5. Fork the rice gently and transfer to a serving dish. Garnish with the roasted coconut.

Spicy Tomato Rice

Serves: 4-5
Time required: 40 minutes (Soaking time: 30 minutes)

INGREDIENTS

2½ cups *basmati* rice
1 cup tomato purée
1 tbsp clarified butter
1 tsp cumin seed
a small stick cinnamon
½ tsp red chilly powder
1 tsp salt
water
2 tomatoes, finely chopped
1 tbsp coriander leaves, freshly chopped

METHOD

1. Put the rice in a sieve and wash thoroughly under running cold water. Soak in plenty of cold water for about 30 minutes. Drain the rice in a sieve and let it stand for a minute or two.
2. Dilute the tomato purée in about ¼ cup water.
3. Heat clarified butter in a large heavy-bottomed saucepan. Add cumin seeds and the cinnamon stick. As soon as the seeds pop, add the diluted purée, red chilly powder and salt.
4. Cook for 1-2 minutes, then add the drained rice. Stir fry for 2 minutes, then level the rice with a spatula and pour enough water to cover the rice by about one inch. Bring to a boil and lower the heat. Cover and cook for about 20 minutes, until the rice is tender and all the moisture has been absorbed.
5. Fork the rice gently and transfer to a heated serving dish. Sprinkle with chopped tomatoes and fresh coriander.

Chinese Fried Rice

Serves: 2
Time required: 40 minutes

INGREDIENTS

1½ cups cooked rice
4 tbsp refined oil
1 bunch spring onions, chopped (discard the leafy area)
100 gm French beans, finely chopped
2 carrots, finely chopped
4 sticks celery, chopped
1 capsicum, chopped
½ tsp Ajinomoto powder (optional)
1 tbsp soy sauce
salt to taste
2 eggs, whisked
1 cup cooked and diced chicken or 1 cup deveined cooked shrimps
3-4 green chillies, chopped and soaked in vinegar
chilly sauce

METHOD

1. Heat oil in a wok. Add the spring onions, French beans, carrots, celery and capsicums. Add Ajinomoto powder. Stir fry on high flame for 3-4 minutes.
2. Add the cooked rice, soy sauce and salt.
3. Pour the egg into the cooked rice and vegetables. Mix very well. Add the chicken and/or shrimps and stir fry for another 2 minutes.
4. Serve hot with green chillies and chilly sauce.

For the happy-go-lucky

(Sandwiches)

For those who are bonny, bright and gay,
There are ribboned sandwiches on a tray.
For those who laugh, as the world goes by,
There are many sandwiches to try.
Happy-go-lucky men are so cheerful
Laughing, friendly and never tearful
Sandwiches are for those gay and happy
And for those who are grey and snappy.
Do try and eat them in a trice
You must, you see, because they are so nice!

Ribbon Sandwich

METHOD

1. Take 3 or more slices of bread. The bread should be ¼-inch thick. Either all white or all brown bread will do. But you also have the option to use them alternately.
2. Trim the edges of the bread slices. Place a portion of any one of the fillings alternately on the bread slices (see recipes for the fillings below).
3. After putting in the filling, wrap the sandwich tightly in a damp cloth and press lightly.
4. Cut into half diagonally just before serving.

RECIPES FOR THE FILLINGS:

Ham and Chicken Ribbons

1. Chop ham, season with salt and moisten with fresh cream.
2. Cook chicken (or turkey) and moisten with mayonnaise.

Pepper Ribbons

1. Chop red and green peppers separately.
2. Wring out in a cheese cloth.
3. Moisten with mayonnaise and use in alternate layers as fillings.

Masala Ribbons

1. Use white and brown bread alternately.
2. Make fillings of moist cottage cheese, seasoned well with mint paste.

Easy Sandwich Fillings

1. Use cream butter plain or season it with honey, grated horseradish, cheese and lemon juice.
2. Use peanut butter plain or moisten it with salad dressing. Add a little sugar or jam.
3. Chop hard-boiled eggs and mix with mayonnaise. Add chopped gherkins (pickled) and season to taste.
4. Moisten chicken chops with mayonnaise. Add chopped celery.
5. Mash shrimps and add seasoning.
6. Mix guava jelly spread with cheese.

7. Mix cheese, anchovy and cream butter with grated cheese, vinegar, salt and pepper. Mix in paprika, mustard and anchovy sauce.
8. Mix skinned and mashed sardines with hard-boiled eggs. Season with cayenne pepper, salt and lemon juice. Moisten with olive oil or butter.
9. Mix tuna (or any flaked white fish) flake with celery and cucumber. Moisten with mayonnaise.
10. Mix grated raw carrots with mayonnaise. Use along with shredded or leafy lettuce.
11. Drain tomato slices and sprinkle French dressing. Dot with mayonnaise.

French Toast Sandwich

METHOD

1. Make sandwiches with fillings of cheese, sliced ham or chicken.
2. Press the slices together firmly.
3. Beat 1 egg slightly and add ¼ cup milk.
4. Dip sandwiches into the egg and milk mixture.
5. Sauté in butter.
6. Garnish, if desired, with crisp bacon.

Open Toasted Cheese Sandwich

METHOD

1. Toast the bread on one side.
2. Place the sliced cheese on the un-toasted side.
3. If desired, top with bits of uncooked bacon and onion rings.
4. Toast under broiler till the cheese melts.
5. Serve with tomato sauce and sweetbreads.

Conclusion

We have tried our best to suggest ways
To make you feel happier on different days.
The categories we made are not steadfast
Choose your recipe first, the category last.
These recipes are brought to you dear Adam
When on your hand you have a sulking madam.
Surprise her with a dish she can't refuse
The lights will go off faster than a fuse!
Tease her with the prowess you develop overnight
She'll concede defeat quickly without a fight!
Show off your cooking with tips from us
The stomach and the ego both need a fuss!
Most importantly, enjoy what you do
Remember cooking is fun for the discerning few!!

INDEX

BORED
PASTA